Forgiving The Unforgivable
Removing the Obstacles to Love

Niramisa Weiss

Eternal love and gratitude to Mum and Dad.

CONTENTS

And now we stand in terror before what we swore never to look upon.
Our eyes look down, remembering our promise to our 'friends'. The
'loveliness' of sin, the delicate appeal of guilt, the 'holy' waxen image of
death, and the fear of vengeance of the liar we swore in blood not to
desert, all rise to bid us NOT to raise our eyes.
For we realise that, if we look on THIS, and LET the veil be lifted,
THEY WILL BE GONE FOREVER.
All of our 'friends', our 'protectors', and our 'home' will vanish.
Nothing that we remember NOW, will we remember.

A Course In Miracles

1 BEGINNINGS

This book started life as a project collaboration idea. At the time, I was deep in the process of writing my first book, *The Liar*. One morning, without warning, around the same time I was drafting chapter eleven, the idea for *Forgiving The Unforgivable* popped into my mind. I felt like shouting, "Eureka!" I was awestruck. We will save the world and forgive everything in it, I thought. And everyone will be desperately keen to be on board, I thought. Pope Francis will forgive the Catholic paedophile priests in one chapter. In another, Aung San Suu Kyi will forgive her people for killing Muslims. In another chapter, Marianne Williamson will forgive corporate America. The Dalai Lama will forgive the Chinese in yet another. *(Thinking big is a great meditation.)* I would do my wee bit, of course, but I wouldn't have *so* much hard work. I thought.

This was great news and I was much relieved as, at that time, I was finding looking so closely at the liar's game a little heavy-going. Still, I was so convinced of the wonder and non-ordinary origin of the new book idea that I registered the copyright immediately and sat it on the back-burner. Once *The Liar* was published and available, I thought, it wouldn't be too long before everyone was knocking at the door desperate for a piece of this forgiving action, I thought.

Well, not so. Well, not so quickly perhaps. But you know what? That's OK. I'll just do the work myself. Having been through the process of writing and publishing *The Liar*, and continuing my work with JC and *A Course In Miracles*, I believe I'm ready for the task. I'm reasonably sober now, as well as extremely joyful and peaceful, and I simply cannot, in all seriousness, condemn anyone for anything anymore. So let's get going shall we?

It must be obvious to everyone by now that the human world is insane. This is not even up for question - no matter how mad we are - because we only have to look at the glaring environmental disasters, constant genocides, or quote hunger statistics versus food surplus to see the situation as it is.

The problem is that, even when we are clear about the self-destructive lunacy of the human race, each and every one of us believes we have escaped this insanity personally. This idea is, of course, part of the same madness we are looking at externally and judging as *evil*, separate, and nothing to do with ourselves. The truth is, we are all suffering from exactly the same insanity, and the insanity is our problem and nothing else. Furthermore, until we take that humble first step and agree that we ourselves are part of the problem, in every situation we find ourselves exasperating over, nothing can change. The belief that our species-wide issues are nothing to do with us personally is never true.

The insane must start to notice their insanity or we are doomed for sure.

Understanding the hellish world we have made for ourselves, and how we unwittingly support it, can lead us to *reasoning* ourselves into peace of mind. This seems rather appealing, particularly for us left-brainers. Intellectual somersaulting around half-understood spiritual texts is more commonly the way we negotiate our way through the mess of our collective thinking, without much luck; never mind the religious nonsense that must be taken on faith, untested. My personal experience of witnessing the liar in the human mind, and closely examining its functioning, has left me with no other choice but to discard any non-peaceful thoughts, simply because they are not true.

By understanding the liar in the human minds, we can forgive everything easily. We can forgive even the most horrible events because there is nothing in our faulty perception bigger or smaller, better or worse, than anything else. The liar's voice governs the majority of our thoughts. We listen to it and believe it mistakenly, without knowing that we do. However, a mistake is just a mistake and, although the effects of our mistakes in the world can be tragic and saddening, condemning each other as *evil* compounds a simple error into a bigger problem, more difficult to fix. The concept of *evil* also springs from this voice of destruction. When we discard the liar in the mind, we have no other option but to write off *evil* as surplus to human requirements.

When we see concepts like *evil* as thoroughly illusory, the way forward becomes clear. We can examine any act we previously thought inexcusable and find an alternative way to understand our fellows and the devastating decisions they made that caused so much upset. We do not condone, but we cannot see any other course of action they could have taken given their circumstances at the time and our now better-understood collective state of insanity.

In Chapter Two, we will recap with a clear description of the liar before embarking on the bulk of the work destined for this book. The focus of the work will be a collection of essays; we might call them proofs by examination of the activities of the liar in the human mind; or research papers that might support the original thesis. We will forgive some of the more dreadful events that have taken place in our world recently; things that have been impossible to understand, leaving us powerless to resolve. Forgiveness, as we usually have it, is a misinterpretation set out by the liar in our minds, and we have accepted its fake definition as de facto. Prior to heading on into the forgiving process, Chapter Three will look at the definition of the forgiveness we all know and cherish, and state the case for redefining it into something more logical, reasonable, and useful.

After these preliminaries, we will travel through specific and general examples of the horrors of the human world. We will understand them in terms of the liar model of perception and there will be no recourse but to forgive the doers of these acts. Our collective consciousness will have escaped the grip of guilt and condemnation. Some of the examples are specific ones I had puzzled over for many years. Others are general cases which reveal how broadly we may apply forgiveness and to any circumstance. There is, of course, much more work to be done that could not be included in this brief inquiry.

We will notice that, although the subject areas appear to vary, we are actually looking at one thing and one thing only. The content of each situation is always the same. The belief that fear is real and must be alleviated in some way underpins every destructive act we have ever known, or will ever know. We will start to see that we ourselves behave in exactly the same way as those we thought we had condemned to an eternity of hell, albeit at lower levels of intensity. Through this compassionate act of honest, fearless, and ruthless self-examination, we will realise that we are all the same, all under the same pressures, all suffering from the same, one, single problem; this liar in the mind.

All the examples are extreme cases of what is going on in everyone's minds, nearly all the time. If we are honest, we will admit it, and then humanity may move on. If not, then the extreme cases will get more extreme - as we are already witnessing - and who knows what we might eventually do to ourselves. It might be sooner than we think, too. We are doing pretty well at whole-scale destruction as it is, and no-one can deny that anymore. Now that we are more interconnected than ever before, the projections of our sick-thinking have become so obvious it should be impossible for us to deny the problem once we have it laid out reasonably and peacefully.

At the beginning of the healing process, the liar will persuade us to avoid taking any responsibility for the chaos in the world. Yet slowly, slowly, we might find ourselves entertaining the notion that we do have a part to play. It might take some big event to flip us into admitting our own conspiracy with the voice of doom; hopefully not though. Common sense and a serious examination of our thinking will leave us unable to deny our own involvement for much longer. We must painstakingly examine our thoughts, discarding deeply-held, deleterious beliefs, one-by-one. Eventually we might even hear this tricky voice, whispering death and destruction to us at every moment. We may realise, joyfully, that we do not have to listen to it or believe it again.

Some of the examples we are going to look at may seem ridiculous to bring up in a book about forgiveness. I point to cases like *homosexuality*, with which most of the saner part of the world has no issue anymore. However, even today, people believe that homosexuality is wrong, a crime, and thus can justify irrational hatred and violence towards other human beings. On the other hand, the fact that many of us have no problem anymore is an excellent example of how the true definition of forgiveness functions. If we cannot fathom why things like suicide, homosexuality, or abortion should appear in a book about forgiveness, we have quietly forgotten our own culture's recent madness completely, as if it never happened. This is cause for hope and this is exactly what we must do in our forgiveness practice.

Each lie we examine, each nasty incident we witness, reveals the same tired, old problem taking yet another ghoulish form in the world. We must look dispassionately in order to see why discarding falsehood is our only sane option. Evidence that our collective perception can change overnight, and definitions of *evil* drift into forgetfulness, is wonderful proof of our ability to forgive and forget. Perhaps the younger generation in the West might be shocked to find out that, nowadays, women are stoned to death in other countries over inconsequential matters. However, it was not so long ago that our own culture's treatment of women was equally appalling.

Gender difference is one of the liar's most powerful distortions. Gender inequality is a lie we all believe at varying levels of intensity, even when we are fully aware of its inherent lunacy. The gender lie is so widespread, so untouchable, and possibly the master key to unlocking all suffering, that I think a closer examination of it should be left to further work. We will not, therefore, look too specifically at gender in this book; although, as it is the biggest lie we cherish, I will have to mention it briefly, here and there. At these challenging moments, we would do well to remember what we used to justify without flinching, as well as what is possible for humans with a shared peace of mind.

Accepting people as they are is nothing but an approach towards an experience of unconditional love. What a person does or believes, if it is not hurting another, is no-one else's business. However, if great numbers of people are prepared to kill or cause suffering to others due to mad beliefs, we must add the underlying ideas to the list of things we need to examine closely, understand, forgive and so discard. We will forgive the thinking that causes such suffering and we will forgive those that entertain the thoughts of destruction, without knowing that they do.

If we find ourselves wondering why we have to forgive gay men, or people who commit suicide, or women who abort babies, we are half way there. However, when we bring in paedophiles, murderers, and rapists into the discussion, the going starts to get a little tough. Yet the only way we will find freedom is to understand why we humans behave as we do. We can understand ourselves by looking very carefully at the thoughts that fuel such actions, and noticing that all regrettable actions stem from false beliefs.

Wherever we feel the most uncomfortable while we are reading this book, is a signal as to where our own personal work might be. However, in forgiving our fellows, we automatically forgive ourselves and so heal our own personal discomfort. Ultimately, forgiveness is the only way we will free ourselves and take the next giant leap forward into a new, limitless, and peaceful experience of life, where one person cannot be better or worse than any other.

The children are walking hurriedly towards the fire, their pace increasing. We are not angry when we forcefully pull the children to safety but if we try to cajole them away from it, or be nice and polite about it - more concerned with not hurting their feelings (the liar in their minds) - we are being dishonest with them and they will miss an important lesson. It is the same situation when dealing with the liar. The liar is behind every upset in the world and has become so sneaky - burying itself deep inside our perception - it has easily managed to obfuscate all blame and project it away from itself. Anytime we approach the liar in the mind, it gets agitated and deflects the issue. We will find ourselves getting irritated and annoyed as we approach the foundations of murder, war, rape, paedophilia, abortion, and genocide.

We will attempt to deflect the problem away from ourselves and onto shadowy figures that do not exist.

Initially, we may even feel terror while walking this path. At these times we should remember how badly we have been fooled, and for how long. Even so, we will want to cover our faces and hide from that which we *must* look at. We may even be cajoled into attacking the person telling us to look, as if all the insanity we cannot deny were their fault alone; as if any of it were of value and worth keeping.

However, what are we truly doing when we get angry, agitated, frustrated, or even obstinately refuse to read a book such as this? Put simply, we are protecting our crazy world as it is. If we take the apathetic attitude with our children as they run towards the fire, they will be irrevocably burnt. Would we take this attitude with our children? If not, why are we taking it with our own species, allowing it to destroy itself, along with ourselves and our children too? Is this what we truly want?

We meander blindly through our lives, believing we are fine and that everyone else is mad. The idea that the problems of the world are someone else's, and not ours, is wrong. The liar orders us to project our guilt on those external to us, thus ensuring our safety. It promises us more safety if we are dishonest and defend our own unhelpful behaviour. However, the liar's definition of safety, and of many other simple and clear concepts, is upside-down and back-to-front. This definition of safety, that apparently protects the one from the dangerous others, is now about to destroy our paradise and all who live on it.

The guilt fuelling the state of the human world rests on everyone's shoulders. Yet we believe we can dump our guilt on another and relieve ourselves of it. Thus, we sleepwalk through the motions of dumping our guilt onto others, remaining blind to our complicity as well as our power to change anything or help anyone. Those we dump our guilt onto believe that it is possible to take on the guilt of others, confirming this bizarre delusional process is real and functioning. But it is all just total hallucination. If we believe we have successfully shifted our guilt onto someone else, and we look carefully inside our minds, we will find the guilt is still there, not a jot removed. That is why the projection of guilt and finger-pointing must continue on, relentlessly, because it will never deliver the result we expect, even though we never doubt it will; a clear proof of insanity.

Furthermore, let's not get caught up in intellectual trickery by asking questions such as why certain horrors happened to him and not her, for example. Asking why something happens to one person and not another is a bit like being seriously concerned as to why a particular leaf is on a particular branch of a tree, and not another. It actually doesn't matter. Things are as they are. Let's deal with situations as we find them and not worry about *what ifs*. In any case, this is just the liar again, asking irrelevant questions in order to lead us up the crazy-paved, garden path. It convinces us that the answers to untold pointless questions are important and so avoids being unveiled, yet again. It does this *a lot*.

Although we have projected into the world our firm belief in separation and isolation, ever since we were able, we have nevertheless reached a state of existence in which our conscious minds can see how much in error we have been. Let's not waste this opportunity. Let's begin the healing of the human mind. There is nothing left to do but forgive everything that has ever happened that continues to haunt us. We will see that true forgiveness brings freedom from the torment we have endured, yet accepted; the world we despair of daily. And it couldn't be easier. We will see how valueless the violent world we thought we wanted actually is.

If you're not in now, if you don't join me now, you can be sure it will be back to *ho-heave-ho* for humans again. Eons more of filth, slavery, and punishment; millions whipped and beaten dragging monster stones up ravines for one random person's liar-pleasure; back-breaking short lives, umpteen pregnancies, poverty and squalor; all this yet again for the next cycle, or something equally insane. Is this a reasonable option for the good and noble human species, the most evolved species on the planet? Let's get ourselves out of the mess while we have this splendid opportunity.

Are you in?

2 WHAT IS THE LIAR IN THE MIND?

Please join me on a thought experiment in which you don't have to believe anything at all; just sit back, enjoy the ride, and exercise your creative thinking a little bit.

If Heaven had a website, how do you think it would look? What sort of pictures would we see on Heaven.com's front page? What type of content and articles might we read and digest? What kind of videos, music, and links could we find on the site? Do you think we would be able to interact with Heaven.com and, if so, how?

It could be miraculous! Imagine! We could communicate with all our loved ones, here or departed, whenever we wanted. We could email the angels, asking for the solutions to our problems directly; an answer received in our mailbox the very moment we asked for help. Wouldn't it be wonderful not to have to rely on belief and faith (against the seeming, worldly, lack of proof) that our prayers might be answered? Maybe we could even communicate personally with The Big G!

Let's imagine, for a moment, that this website exists. Heaven.com has beautiful, soft, and unearthly music playing and a virtual garden so exquisite that wandering around it, albeit hypothetically, makes us feel like we have always belonged there, existing in peace and joy; just, so, happy and content. Unusual, colourful, and friendly creatures roll at our feet as rose petals drift about. We meet and greet all the others in this electronic reality as if they were our long lost, beloved brothers and sisters, all difficult histories completely forgotten.

At the Heaven.com website there is no inequality. Everyone loves and is loved equally, and there is no pain and suffering. Limitless creativity is the order of the day and users of the website may find themselves doing all sorts of amazing things not limited by everyday physical laws. Furthermore, all of us have full, unlimited, and free membership for eternity, regardless of who we are and what we may have done in our lives.

Now.

Imagine hackers have infiltrated the server on which Heaven.com is managed. They have successfully placed a nasty software virus between what the creator of the website intended and our own personal computers connected to the Internet. The virus functions by searching for anything that might be innocent, pleasing, loving, kind, soft, quiet, and peaceful, and painting onto it a shadowy, destructive overlay so that it becomes ugly and distorted.

Heaven.com is rendered unrecognisable. The once-exquisite gardens have become a radioactive, toxic, landfill site. The angels have turned into evil criminals, brandishing knives and guns, drooling for blood and money. The beautiful creatures start to die horrible, painful deaths in their millions; whole species wiped out by the minute. The sidebar articles that had described continual peace, joy, and love tell gruesome horror stories, all with a running theme of how everyone is in peril and at risk of injury, illness, pain, and death at any moment.

There is an excess of information on the site about how we should all be very concerned about the certainty of attack, robbery, and murder by an unidentifiable group of sinister folk with very bad intentions. The definition of these unknown assailants shifts endlessly, dependent on our personal experience; so they could be the criminally insane, the government, squatters, or a group of elderly ladies. The soft music has turned into grunge metal, or Justin Bieber maybe. Hmm, already sounds like somewhere we are all too familiar with, doesn't it?

Well, this is the liar.

The liar is a human perceptual virus, obscuring reality. It repaints everything good, kind, connected, and loving as evil, malicious, and fearsome. The liar, alone, builds the world of which we despair. A world in which we believe we are completely isolated, lost, afraid, and viciously pitted against the other fearful beings here, those we are sure are intent on doing us harm. This dark filter over the truth takes different forms for different people, usually dependent on life experience, but the content of the messages it sends is always the same: *Be afraid, be very afraid.*

For example, a person who was brought up by parents who had, in their past, been robbed of their business and livelihood, might inherit a belief that everyone is out to take what belongs to them. This unquestioned belief could affect every decision they make in their lives, without them being aware of it. Examples like this are not rare cases. We are crippled by the belief that we are constantly about to be robbed. We only have to look at the news to have it proved to us on a daily basis. Indeed, all our personal *belongings* are at risk of *theft*; such as our precious time, the attention we expect from loved ones, and the respect we are undoubtedly due from everyone else, to name just a few examples of our cherished possessions we are sure someone will rip from our hands.

The most interesting thing about these fearful ideas is that the liar insists we act first, before the inevitable happens; a defence before the counted-upon attack. Thus, we who believe that others are going to take what is rightfully ours, attempt to avert such onslaughts by attacking first, in the same way. When these ideas are examined carefully, the madness of their circularity is clearly seen. We also see the fact that what we fear the most is exactly how we behave ourselves. This is enlightening. We would have to go back to the beginning of time to find out who started any of it. All this occurs due to the liar in our minds, convincing us of the fearful nature of the world and the need to attack it first before we become its prey. This is why it is so easy for politicians to justify war to a fearful populace.

We all believe we are vulnerable at some level - singularly and in groups. Fear of attack admits this belief because if we were sure of our power there would be no fear of attack. The liar doesn't allow us a nanosecond to consider this peaceful notion. Thus, we have defined strength as physical strength alone; specifically in terms of how effective such strength is in overpowering the others who are about to attack us. We fail to see that a definition of strength that relies on an admittance of personal weakness is an oxymoron.

I have already published a full explanation of the insanity of the liar in the human mind and how it operates, looking at a range of aspects of our perceptual experience as human beings on planet Earth at the current time. In the book, I explain how this software-virus-like error in thinking controls the minds of humans and produces everything of which we despair. It is astonishing to see the scope of the liar's influence. Nothing in the human world - no system, no organisation, area of study, human necessity, pastime, person, or idea - is free from its infection.

From the moment we enter this world, the voice of destruction defines our experiences. With the most basic separation notion of *I am here, and you are over there*, the liar persuades us of the reality of fearfulness, and the certainty of attack and punishment. *Because you are over there*, it says, *you are my enemy*, it says. You will surely want to take what is mine, and you are bound to attack me for it, so I had better attack you first, and call it defence. From these first fearful thoughts, in the minds of the tiniest of toddlers, the human world forms.

The liar's voice has roots so deep in our perception, we think it is our own true voice, and so we identify with it, believing its destructive ideas are our own. Misidentifying with the liar in the mind is the only way we could do the dreadful things we do in this world, because we believe this lunatic voice which is intent on our destruction, while we have no idea that it is there. We do not know what we are doing because we are fast asleep, on auto pilot, obeying a dictator that moulds our perception. This dictator points to those of us who have obeyed it assiduously to devastating effect, and labels them *evil* and condemned to hell. This voice we think is our own will betray us at any moment.

The liar in our mind uses anything it can to convince us to destroy each other and ourselves. Onto an unemotional and unbiased description of anything in the world, it adds its own judgment by labelling it good or bad, beneficial or useless, good for getting something for ourselves or worthless for our own personal goals, about to attack or needing attack, and on and on. This dualistic labelling process is the foundation of judgment and we may label anything at all. Hence, bizarre wars are fought on the most ridiculous concepts, such as a preference for a particular label representing God, for example.

We become enraged when our self-definitions are attacked; definitions formed by false labels we have believed to be true. We are willing to kill to defend them, even ourselves at times. However, it is not *we* who feel the rage. It is, in fact, this liar we have identified with which thrives on conflict and its attempts to incite it, whenever and however it can. The liar uses anything that separates us in a physical or mental sense to justify judgments of worse-than or better than against an elusive and shifting standard that the liar defines and redefines. Skin colour, body shape and size, genital type, IQ level, how much money we have or don't have, where we live, what job we do, our accent, which team we support, which newspaper we read; all these things are used to define the others over there as worse than, or better than, ourselves.

Judgment goes on, and judgment can only exist due to better-than, worse-than labels and beliefs. We can be sure that, sooner or later, the worse-than label will arrive back at our door. If we look very closely at our thoughts, we see that any better-than judgment is actually hiding a more persistent worse-than, no matter how successful - by the world's standards - we are. Judgment is the liar's game, maintaining separateness and differences, and giving us cause to believe we are better than the rest. This *betterness* briefly alleviates our deeper sadness and slightly more honest fearfulness; that which we cannot bear to face directly. Thus, somehow, the liar does us a favour by diverting our attention from what truly troubles us; the deep wound in our hearts that has us split off from each other, causing us to hate even those closest to us, more often *especially* those closest to us.

We must examine our thoughts if we are to have peace. Although we must admit that equality is reasonable and sane, and slowly we are making changes to the way we think and the world is finding equilibrium, irrational judgment still goes on. Moreover, if we have managed to discard false beliefs about other races, or a person's sexual orientation, for example, we have certainly not yet managed to discard false beliefs about the body, or gender, or personal relationships, or how much money we have, or what food we should eat, or our health; the list is endless.

The liar redefines destructive ideas in order to convince us of their appeal. It doesn't stop there either. It also redefines peaceful ideas in order to render them unappealing. It does this to maintain its dominant position in our thought processes. It is very sneaky indeed. As we have seen, it re-labels attack with defence, and so justifies attack. It re-labels weakness with strength and so justifies violence and war. It calls wealth poverty, and so justifies theft of all varieties, as well as our insane mental attachments to random material objects. Furthermore, it ensures an inability to be satisfied, no matter how much money or objects have been amassed. It calls wisdom foolishness and manages to silence the few sane voices that talk of peace. It calls the truth lies, in order to protect itself. It malevolently redefines the obvious ad nauseam and, bizarrely, we never notice.

The liar must maintain its dominance in our minds and so it does everything it can to avoid being revealed, and consequently discarded. By confusing just about everything that might save us with something unpleasant, it has forced us unwitting humans, in very large numbers, into a planetary situation which has, most recently, become rather perilous. We are currently witnessing the liar in the human mind at its most successful.

If you find it hard to believe this thought-virus is controlling your mind, I know you will have definitely seen it in action at least once in your life, without knowing what it was. You will remember a moment when you had an outrageous and violent thought about someone or something. This thought was so foreign to your regular thinking, you noticed it immediately. The thought passed away and you quickly forgot about it. You reasoned it a rare, if unpleasant, anomalous idea, dismissed it entirely and carried on with your life. This dreadful idea came from the liar and this is where it attempts to take us all. Sadly, some of us are thinking thoughts as extreme as these continuously; struggling to dissociate from them.

We will see that the question is not why a person did what they did; the question is, instead, what caused them to believe the liar's voice at extremes when most people do not. The answer to this is excruciating levels of fear, provoking similarly excessive reactions in the hope of escape from the fear. However, no-one is immune to the continuous dictates of the liar in the mind, and any extreme violence the liar may dream up is just a more intense version of the destructive thoughts we are all having, moment to moment, however peaceful our lives seem from the outside.

Another area where we can see the liar's ideas very clearly is within close personal relationships. When we are honest with ourselves, we see that our personal beliefs about our partner and loved ones shift constantly from better-than to worse-than; sometimes in the blink of an eye. These shifting beliefs establish our words and actions within our relationships. We believe we love our partner, our children, our parents, but find ourselves full of rage when they act outside our expectations. We do not know what love is and, instead, spend our lives giving and receiving conditional love, then hate, then more conditional love, then hate again, repeated interminably; and this is what we call normal relationships.

The world of the liar is our world.

The liar must disprove the unity of human beings, at all costs. Disproving unity starts with judgment. We judge each other to be good or bad, better or worse, pleasant or horrible, and the fact that we are judging at all means we do not believe in the unity and equality of the human race, or indeed all life. When unity becomes reasonable, the liar's days are numbered. It is well aware of this too. This is why we humans tend to murder those peaceful souls who make great steps towards uniting and healing humanity; and for no other reason at all. The liar must eliminate all opponents.

Cold and unemotional, the liar's judgment is never fixed. There is no truth or stability in the liar's world. You will notice that what you believe to be better, someone else is sure is worse. This disagreement alone may justify conflict and war. You will notice that what you once thought was better, is now worse. There is no definitive, unequivocal truth in the liar's world, and there never will be, by definition.

14

Occasionally we catch a glimpse of what lies behind this miserable, dark, and heavy filter over reality. Heaven.com hasn't gone anywhere actually and these glimpses give us hope. However, the world of the liar is difficult to pierce through, as its ideas are so engrained in everything we have assumed to be true and worth killing to defend.

The root of our insanity is very clever indeed and manages to persuade us that we do not need to change; aside from the obvious fact that everything in this world is in constant flux and we can indeed rely on that. Yet, bizarrely and arrogantly, we humans think we have made it already, that we are at the top of the evolutionary tree with nothing more left to do; ignoring the fact that we are seriously problematic, presenting violent behaviour beyond all reasonability, and are now at the point of destroying our own home. Pointing the blame for our own mess away from ourselves is the basis of our psychological complex and so we look outside, expecting to find an objective, stand-alone truth external to us that will explain our predicament, or save us. We never will.

The overwhelming majority of our thoughts are liar fuelled and all the horrific things that humans do to each other are due to these thoughts not our own. Therefore we, *the real we*, the human being without the liar is, in truth, completely free of blame. Nevertheless, as long as the liar controls our minds we will find ourselves, with some regularity, at the brink of destroying ourselves as a species. If not with the insane weapons we concoct, it might be from the environmental disaster we cause by focusing on our own selfish and illusory desires against all other concerns. As a goal - and one which is worryingly reasonable to the majority of us - *profit over all other considerations* has engendered systems that control the world that have no responsibility to anyone or anything. The liar's systems and organisations are now totally out of control, as well as hell-bent on destruction, as is anything arising from the tenet of separation and isolation.

When we follow the logical process of a belief in separateness and differences, we see the inevitability of the world as it is. The better-than, worse-than thought-system we all agree with, half-asleep, is so insane that even if we became the winner of the game we believe to be reality, it would never be enough; not that this winning state is possible in reality, but that's the insane goal we have accepted without question. The liar's goal is total destruction, so if we happened to be the winner, on our own, and there was no life left to attack us, and we owned everything there was to own, we would have to start splitting our own selves up, pitting some parts against others, just so the warring and conflict could continue. This deeper, more intense application of separation-psychosis is exactly what happens in the minds of those labelled by medics as insane. What we presume to be unquestionably insane is, in fact, just an extreme version of how all our minds are malfunctioning day to day.

Can you imagine a hypnotist's show where one of the volunteers acts like a chicken every time he hears the trigger word? This is the human world. Can we blame the poor volunteers (us) for the things that we do unwittingly under such pathetic suggestion? Would this sort of condemnation stand up in court? The liar is just a sham hypnotist, and we are all fast asleep and doing its bidding.

Life with the liar is sad, limited, small, and hopeless. All the goals it tells us are worth achieving in life ensure loss and the eventual destruction of ourselves and our home. These goals that we cherish have no value in any sense, but we chase after them relentlessly; more proof of the liar's upside-down world of which we are completely unaware but, nevertheless, fervently uphold.

The liar's ideas are meaningless. We can say, in general, that their main characteristics are smallness, conflict-inducing, and completely irrational when examined closely. We should not be concerned with liar thoughts at all. Even their characteristics are not concerns as such, but noticing them helps us to see exactly what we are dealing with. *And this we do need to know.* In fact, if something is part of the human world, we can guarantee the liar is in control of it at some level. Now we know what this liar is and how it functions, we have a chance to stop believing it and watch it dissipate into nothing. Disbelieving the liar effectively unplugs it from its energy source, silencing it immediately.

Anything that can shift state into its opposite at any given nanosecond, dependent on which state will be the most destructive at that particular moment, is clearly delusional and unstable. Understanding the liar's workings strips it of its reasonability and reveals its insanity. Moreover, madness does not invite condemnation. What madness invites, is crying out for, is healing and peace of mind.

Whatever our world is without the liar can be compared to Heaven.com because everything unpleasant and harmful in our world is liar-made. Life without the liar has to be something wonderful, something worth making an effort for, something we would be happy to leave as a legacy for the generations to come, instead of the burgeoning nightmare we have endured for so long. This is new and uncharted territory, ready for human discovery; the peaceful and loving world within.

By comparing the liar to a computer virus, I have, I hope, described a way to understand what it is and how it functions. There is, however, no computer code for the liar. There are no switches working machines that process each of its instructions either. It is just a crazy idea; rather like a cloud formation, ready at any moment to shift into something else, fade, and then disappear. Currently, this shadowy cloud formation has total control over life on Earth, but this will change. We will see our problem and begin to discard it. Eventually, we won't even remember these horrible times. There will be no liar in our minds, because there never was one. It was all just a dream we believed to be real.

3 REDEFINING FORGIVENESS

How can we condemn a person to eternal damnation when we are aware, without doubt, that they were not in their right mind when they did what they did? We do not find it difficult to accept the mental disorders of - and so act compassionately towards - the profoundly insane. The formal label *insane* allows us to view people as sick and so lacking genuine responsibility for their actions. If we could see that we are all similarly insane, the only difference being in the form and intensity of the expression of our shared insanity, we would not be able to maintain the reality of *evil* or sure punishment in hell for anyone.

None of us has any real control over our lives or the decisions we make, and understanding what the liar is leads us to this realisation. Ignorance of the liar and its activities in our minds, means that we have had to insist that abhorrent crimes are committed due to no other reason than an inherent *badness* we acquire at birth, whether we like it or not. This bizarre idea is so irrational and problematic it requires a great deal of support in order to be accepted. One such support, the notion of *evil*, popped up in our minds, way, way back in the past and we welcomed it wholeheartedly.

We gave *evil* further sanctioning and support with monsters, devils, demons and malicious powers, all with an undoubted external existence, and ready and waiting to attack. Nowadays, in our brave new, scientifically-minded world, such devils are inadmissible due being unavailable for microscopic analysis; but the belief in *evil* persists and, thus, still requires support. Thus, apart from the obvious labelling of those we fear as *evil*, whether it is our next door neighbour or the dark-skinned ones living a long way away, we should not be surprised that scientific researchers spend time and money chasing down the *evil* gene, and other such pursuits, in order to explain the problem away. This time-wasting serves other purposes too, in that evidence for an *evil* gene, or similar, would prove definitively that some of us are worse than us better-than ones; but more importantly that we are defined by our bodies alone, as if consciousness were an irrelevant quirk of humans; more tail-chasing after proof of the liar's crazy foundations.

Evil is the subject of so much endless, circular debate that never gets us anywhere. The truth is that, with the liar controlling our minds, we are not aware of anything we do, let alone why we do it, and we have not solved any of our problems yet. Our troubles just shift into different forms, growing bigger, more intricate, inclusive, and convoluted. The forms our problem has taken now are now approaching cataclysmic status.

So, apart from minor temporary gains towards peacefulness, and even though it appears we have personal choice and are able to make decisions by ourselves, all anyone is doing is perpetuating destructiveness to a greater or lesser degree. If we are aware of the liar, we can see that the only choice we have ever had is whether to be *more* intensely destructive, or to maintain the current level of misery we have accepted as normal in our lives. The liar requires suffering, pain, destruction, separation, isolation, drama, and tragedy for its existence, and so it offers us life experiences that will keep us enslaved to these ideas.

Our will is completely imprisoned and, yet, we have no idea that it is. We do not know what we humans do and so far - apart from the odd one or two of us - we have never known. Free will cannot be properly exercised while an unseen dictator controls our minds. We are all slaves, in fact. The slave trade itself is nothing compared to what every single human being is enduring on this planet constantly, without knowing it. And, bizarrely, we are each of us our own slave-master because the power is ours to stop believing the liar in the mind at any moment and so free ourselves. In those instances in which we consciously ignore the liar, we notice that its voice fades away into nothing without fuss. The liar has no real substance at all, just like *evil*. Choosing to stop listening to the liar will end our involuntary requirement for conflict and will be the beginning of an authentic experience of free will.

Our chosen slave-master does a great job of painting a dark and fearsome picture of true freedom. This is so we avoid is assiduously. We have *fallen in love* with our captor and are convinced that its destructive whims are our personal pleasures. We believe our crazy lives are reasonable and that we are doing our best under the impossible circumstances we see around us, but not within us. We haven't noticed that whatever we want for ourselves, and whatever we put immense energy into acquiring, is that which causes us dullness and pain. We believe addictions, romance, sex, power, money, and ownership of people, things, status, and knowledge are that which will provide happiness and yet, undeniably, they never do. We rarely notice we are never satisfied, never fulfilled. It is like slamming our heads violently against a brick wall in order to relieve the pain of doing so and - after wondering why it didn't work for a moment - trying it again, and again, perpetually.

The alcoholic who is unaware of having a problem does not see himself as suffering. On the contrary, he is convinced that his life is completely normal. Those around him cannot help but notice his nonsensical attempts at rationalising this insanity, sometimes by bizarre and illogical projections of his own unconscious guilt onto innocent others. Nevertheless, nothing he says or does changes the fact that he is enduring appalling pain and misery, without permitting himself the awareness of it. Even the daily monster-hangovers are not unpleasant enough to do anything about. It is not just the alcoholic behaving this way. This is how we all behave, in endlessly varying forms. Sometimes the form our insane behaviour takes is horrific and tragic, and sometimes just foolish but, whatever the form and intensity, the content is no different from that of the unaware alcoholic, crooked politician, or proud corporate defender of profit over all other considerations. All of us are blind to our own self-destructive tendencies.

We have yet to notice that fear informs our every experience in this world and is accepted as completely normal, never questioned. We assume we are in control of our lives and we are convinced we have a choice between right and wrong, better and worse. We do not see that the only choice available to us in any situation is stasis or even more suffering. We cannot see that everything we do, no matter how good our intentions, supports the continuance of this human world of misery and pain that we have never been able to change, no matter how vigorously we debate it.

We believe we are operating singly, on our own, with no influence from anything outside us, and that this is the state of freedom; separate human bodies acting autonomously, able to compete and win against the others. The notion of unity with all life is never considered because this is an idea the liar fears immensely. It must obscure any suggestion of human unity and equality. It tells us that unity would mean we are equal to the paedophile, rapist, mass murderer, and our best friend; and we must certainly avoid that because we are, of course, much, much better than those *evil* ones.

Like accepting the daily hangovers as reasonable, we decide that unity must be madness, rationalise the suffering we have now as reasonable, and rarely think about it. The freedom that will come from the equality we sometimes hear about, then, appears to be giving up singularity, separateness, and autonomy; that which we believe is our dominance, powerfulness, and divine right. This couldn't be further from the truth.

We are all completely mad. The alcoholic's predicament mirrors our own. We never consider that the insane, tormented world we put up with is fundamentally in error and so, by addressing the symptoms and effects of our madness alone, we have never found a durable solution to any suffering in the world. Even when our personal share of suffering is severe, we become inured to it, accepting it as normal and carrying on with our lives as if we knew where and what we are. The fact is that we are all in the same boat, none of us with a paddle, all of us complaining bitterly about our predicament, yet resolutely unwilling to do anything about it. However, if we all have the same problem, then unity and equality must be valid.

The liar tells us we are separate and individual, and that we must never share anything with anyone in order to maintain our better-than-ness, and we accept the idea. Yet this is nonsense, and we can see it quickly and easily when we look carefully enough. This not-sharing ethic, assumed to be the driving force for human activity, is now depressingly wrecking our beautiful home and we are certainly going to share our experience of that. The truth is we share everything; ironically, especially when we have had some success in attaining the presumed meaning of life of *lone winner* who owns everything. A human driven to extreme acts of destructiveness due to loneliness and fear based upon separation and lack of unity with others, shares their pain with us all. We share everything, especially our insanity and all its effects. But we will share the healing of it too.

The baton of suffering is passed around and we may have helped ourselves to a giant portion, or just a regular amount, but we will all take some. The liar swirls and rebuilds itself in newly arriving minds, grotesque ideas gaining momentum and power, forced along by indisputable acceptance or attack on the tiniest whiff of transgression; and just like a black hole, the liar's business sucks us all in, powerless, pulling us steadily closer to self-annihilation. We even give these processes of the liar - which we have not failed to notice, albeit sleepily - philosophical, economical, and psychological definitions and labels, as if any of it were reasonable and sane.

If we can agree that we are *like* the alcoholic in denial, with our own version of the same suffering, however subtle that might be, then an even better way of seeing this would be that we *are* the alcoholic in denial, the denial has just taken another form. Equally, we *are* the rapist, the paedophile, and the mass murderer; the problem for these unfortunate people just appears different to our personal representations of it. This healing idea comes from a belief in the reality of our conscious connection and the acceptance of a unified human mind. The problem, itself, is always the same, whatever the effects. Lies.

Having described the liar and shown that it is in control of everything we think and do, it follows logically that the definition of forgiveness is something it would be very keen to ensure meets its own goals. Thus, just like the definitions for strength, passion, joy, and wealth which the liar has reworked into meaninglessness by reinterpreting as weakness, suffering, pain, and poverty, so it has further ensured that whatever we think forgiveness is maintains the belief in the inherent *badness* of human beings. This safeguards its own survival.

In the same way a prosthetic leg is only required if a person has actually lost a leg, forgiveness is only required when we believe that whatever happened was *evil* and deserves condemnation. Forgiveness is balm for the suffering, hatred, and anger incited by having condemned and blamed a person for doing something *bad*. However, *bad* things occur due to minds in torment, acting to save themselves from exaggerated levels of fearfulness. Given that condemnation comes from minds which have not yet witnessed the liar, and so continue to believe in the existence of *evil*, we can say that forgiveness - as we are familiar with it - is part of the liar's world and therefore doesn't exist either. Forgiveness is certainly unnecessary outside the liar's system of thought.

The ripples of suffering that vicious acts cause make us sad and regretful. However, we forgive the act itself and not the ripples. The ripples of suffering we can deal with, as long as we don't believe the guilt was transferred successfully onto *victims* and others. For example, the victims of a serial killer don't suffer guilt in the same way as the victims of a rapist. This is because, currently, we consider victims of sexual abuse guilty of the crime as well. This, again, is due to the liar's activities in that its ideas are, currently, weighted towards maintaining the better-than state of the perpetrator's label. This weighting is actually entirely arbitrary. Yet our belief in illogical guilt being successfully passed around is a confusing red-herring, so we will look at it more closely in a later chapter where it will make a lot more sense by example.

Forgiveness belongs to the liar's world, and has been defined by it and from within it. That is why we find it as difficult to forgive our best friend something minor and inconsequential as we do a more hardened criminal something devastating. In truth, there is no difference between the two perceptual shifts required for peace of mind. If we have condemned anyone for anything, then forgiveness makes sense and is required for peace of mind. However, could anyone possibly achieve the promised peace of forgiveness when it is part and parcel of the liar's world? The liar ensures we have a big struggle with this.

Given that we cannot seriously condemn insane behaviour, rather than struggling with forgiving the condemned we could instead step back and lift the condemnation by noticing our shared madness - an illness indeed. When we see that none of us know what we do, we will find ourselves unable to condemn each other any longer. Once condemnation is seen to be an essential part of the liar's definition of reality, and therefore to be discarded along with it, there will be no more need for its version of forgiveness either. This is the shift we make when we fully understand what the liar is.

The forgiveness we are familiar with says, *Oh well, you did this very bad thing, but that's OK, you have been in prison or we chopped something off, or whatever, so we'll let you out now, but YOU WILL ALWAYS HAVE DONE THIS VERY BAD THING.* That is the world's forgiveness. The *evil* that made us do the *very bad thing* remains within and will always be there, ready to reappear at any moment. The wrongdoer is tarnished forever, no matter how much punishment they may have endured, or how long ago the *evil* took place. Moreover, we are tarnished along with him, by holding onto our own share of the *evil* in the form of continued hatred and condemnation.

If we cannot see things as they truly are, then forgiveness, regardless of honest intention, has to be a perceptual leap of faith or intellectual somersaulting; confused at best, repetition of poorly-understood platitudes at worst. When we are honest with ourselves, we see that peace of mind is impossible to achieve under these restrictions. If we fail to see things as they are, then our perception remains hooked into the world's faulty reasoning, so this somersaulting and obstacle-coursing our way into forgiveness is most often very difficult. It usually falters, and, at least, needs continuous reapplication because it is not secure. This forgiveness arises from the same madness from which we

24

are trying to free ourselves. Attempting forgiveness under these constraints can feel like trying to wrench ourselves free from a bear-trap; pretty unpleasant.

Redefining forgiveness means acquiring a way of thinking in which forgiveness, as we have known it, is not necessary at all. We do not condemn, but understand instead. It is a simple change of mind from believing that the world we have is reasonable although regrettable, to realising that all humans are suffering from a severe case of perceptual psychosis. Understanding this is bound to lead to true forgiveness and peace, in a logical and reasonable manner.

Condemnation requires vengeance and punishment, and perpetuates a never-ending circle of irrational misery. Forgiveness, as the liar has it, is necessary only after condemnation. Forgiveness, up until now, has required condemnation. This is a wonderful example of the liar's upside-down world. The only way this sort of forgiveness can bring us peace is together with an unbending faith in the innocence of humanity; but this lucky state of mind is rare. Without this faith, perhaps our forgiveness practice becomes more concerned with maintaining our piety and goodness in the eyes of others, the liar's importance again. Whatever the liar's form of forgiveness is, it is irrational, unreasonable, and virtually impossible for the majority of us, but we have accepted this definition, even though it has never done us much good at all.

Looking more closely, we see that punishment underpins the liar's version of forgiveness; the attempt to fix a wrong by causing another wrong. Sneakily, the liar has built a perpetual guilt machine without us realising it; more circular reasoning, because any intention of harm upon another human being requires more forgiveness at some level. Thus, no real forgiveness is ever achieved, *evil* remains a reality, and hell is the promised future we all believe we deserve, without realising we are already there. The liar's form of forgiveness is something that has no benevolent function, as we might expect. Furthermore, the more formal forms of punishment that exist in our world simply reflect, at the collective level, what is going on in our personal relationships, as we punish each other, condemn and forgive (but not really forgive) repeatedly.

When we see what the liar is, and how it is behind everything in this world that is at the point of imploding, we notice that forgiveness is completely unnecessary, a perceptual leap we might need to work at a little. Nevertheless, I foresee a time in which, like the flat-world becoming round, our true innocence is completely unquestionable. In the meantime, there is no other work worth doing. So let's have a look at some of the horrors we cannot understand. Instances in which we have, in ignorance, condemned our brothers to hellish punishments and an eternity of damnation - and by doing so condemned ourselves and all humanity as well. Let's compassionately see that we would have done *exactly* the same as they, given the same circumstances, resources to hand, and the same cherished, destructive ideas coming from the same mental aberration we all share.

The biggest threat to the liar is its antitheses; truth, innocence, and a belief in the inherent goodness and purity of all life, everything that it is not. It must destroy anything that might prove its falseness and so it will attempt to obliterate any example of innocence, truth, and unconditional love. We only do its bidding because of its promise that we will be less fearful for having done so. At the same time, its bidding insists on the destruction of its enemy, truth. Because truth is what we are, in doing the liar's work, we agree to destroy ourselves.

What we are, behind the fear and psychosis, is the liar's archenemy. It must not let us see this. This is why we sleepily crucified Christ, assassinated Gandhi, murdered Martin Luther King and others, and this is why innocent children are prey for the liar, and for no other reason at all. The liar's screaming gets fever-pitched in the presence of innocence and it persuades us to act appallingly. This is the reality of our mental-slavery. We must become aware of it because when we do so we will never give the voice of doom the same value again. It wants us dead, the real us, the beings that we truly are; the innocent, beautiful, playful, joyful, happy us. Furthermore, death is the liar's only promise on which we can rely.

We are all complicit in the liar's upkeep. It points at the *guilty*, telling us we should rip them to shreds for what they did; all the while knowing very well that the ideas it is propounding - albeit ideas with less impact than what we may be looking at - are exactly the same as those which caused our fellow human to do what he did. We may cry and wail about paedophiles, not noticing our hypocrisy as we sexually objectify our tiny children. We may cry and wail about rapists, not noticing our own hypocrisy as we indulge ourselves in violent, pornographic books and films. We may cry and wail about genocide, not noticing our hypocrisy in that there is at least one race of humans we save for damnation in our own minds, never mind the disappearing species from the natural world. We cry and wail about environmental disaster, not noticing our hypocrisy as we buy and use things that actively cause the destruction of life on Earth, ourselves included. We are all complicit, we are all involved, and we are all taking part in *all* of the madness; and for that reason we all need to heal our minds in order to save ourselves, no exceptions.

No-one can avoid the inevitable healing process. The only thing we can do is delay it. Why bother wasting any more time on violence and hatred? Haven't we had enough now?

True forgiveness is total peace with everything. We might look out at the liar's world and see the chaos in it while understanding it to be just a dream and so remain peaceful within ourselves. On the way to this state of mind, keeping aware will be a daily challenge. We must be certain that no-one is responsible for actions provoked by insane thinking. We must keep in mind that all the horrors of the world come from the seductive persuasion of a lunatic voice inside our heads - a voice of which we are unaware. From here, we will be unable to blame others or defend the notion of *evil*. We will be unable to apparently forgive but never forget again. It's time to undo the knots of guilt and condemnation in our collective perception and envision a future for humanity which we would be happy to leave as a legacy for the coming generations.

All we have to do is remember that any belief that hurts or causes fear does not come from our true selves. Moreover, that no-one is to blame for anything.

Now, let's get to work.

4 WHEN CHILDREN MURDER CHILDREN

All of us have seen the liar in action. We see it regularly in another person, or a group of people, and happily label them *evil* for it. We say, *I can't believe some people*, and then tell a story about how awful these people are, assured that they are undoubtedly far worse than we would ever be. Yet this is madness, because the liar is as deeply entrenched in our own minds as it is in everyone else's, forcing us to behave in the same unpleasant manners we more quickly notice in others. Moreover, only the liar points at other people's behaviour in this supercilious manner, however insignificant or not the behaviour might be.

We rarely notice the liar in our own minds, even though it is there to witness at all times. However, we will all remember a moment in which we had a strong desire to end the life of another person. If we are honest with ourselves, we will admit to feeling this way about a lot of people, continuously, albeit at a lower intensity. *If only that person would go away and not be in my world anymore, life would be better*, we repeat to ourselves, day after day, never thinking once that this unhappy thought might not be justified.

It is amazing that we are only aware of the liar's activities in other people, as if we were the sole good person in all of existence; but it is not surprising given the level of our insanity. When we know what the liar in the mind is, we may notice that we support its doctrine in ourselves while condemning it in others, sometimes in the same breath. Yet regardless of its capacity to evade capture by seeming to only exist externally, no-one is without some personal proof of its presence inside the mind.

As we have already mentioned, we will all have been aware of the liar's voice, at least one time in our lives, even if just momentarily. We will have heard it yelling something so destructive, so shocking, so alien to our normal, daily thought patterns, we could not ignore it. A thought of such extreme vileness passed through our minds, we could hardly believe it was there. In fact, whenever we notice thoughts like these, we pass them over as being nothing to do with us. We give them their true value, i.e. nonsense, and rarely consider them again. We might wonder briefly where such ideas could have come from, but then we forget. These are the rare moments we all have had, now and then, of detachedly witnessing the liar in action, realising its meaninglessness and ignoring it entirely. Remembering these moments is a very useful thing indeed, as it reveals how easy it is to overcome the liar's ideas.

When fear levels are high, extremely destructive ideas can become reasonable. We may identify with the liar's more pernicious notions and consider them as unquestionably our own true thoughts. The extreme pressures that cause overt mental imbalance come from varying forms of acute fearfulness. This fear promotes irrational decision making, founded on the desperate need to escape the same fear, a catch 22. When our minds lose their regular and relatively manageable instability, we may become unable to pass surprisingly vile thoughts over as nothing to do with us personally anymore. If we believe that the liar's intensely violent and destructive ideas are our own, our words and actions may become lamentable too. It is the personal identification with the destructive ideas of the liar, and the inability to dismiss them as nonsense anymore, that cause us to act harmfully.

The horrible murder in February 1993 of baby James Bulger, carried out by two 10 year old boys, is undoubtedly the most heart-breaking crime committed in the UK in recent decades. James, aged 2, was abducted, tortured, and murdered by Robert Thompson and Jon Venables in Merseyside in the North of England. The toddler was last seen on cameras led away from a shopping centre where he had been with his mother that day. His mutilated body was found on a railway line two days later. Thompson and Venables were charged with the abduction and murder of James and, at the same time, the British press and public started screaming for blood and retribution, and they haven't stopped doing so since.

Everyone who hears this sorry story has strong feelings about it, and how could we not? It bothered me for years; something remaining so unresolved about it. We have yet to deal with it in the collective psyche also, as it reappears to haunt us again on a regular basis. There was always something immensely disturbing about two small boys sitting in the dock, their seats raised up in order that their little faces might be seen over the edge of this judicial contraption built for much bigger people; two small children sent down for murder in the same way as a responsible adult.

There is something even more disturbing perhaps about the British public's baying for blood that has not dissipated over 20 years later. It seems as if the only way we can be free of this appalling business is by ripping into shreds the bodies of these two, or of their parents, or of anyone that might be involved with them, in the same way the boys did with James's body. This is the liar's form of forgiveness, an eye for an eye, a body for a body, and such actions have not solved a single problem yet, because if they did we would have done away with the need for them a long, long time ago.

When we look more closely at the lives of these two little boy murderers, we see the indubitable signs of extreme levels of fearfulness coming from profound experiences of lack of love in their short lives. They were both extremely troubled and had already known suffering of a variety which, thankfully, most of us never have any real experience, outside of what we see on TV shows, films, and the Internet, or read in books and magazines. Deciding to steal a tiny child away from his mother to torture, beat, and eventually murder, was an act born of years of abuse, lack of love from parents, and the continued witnessing of violence in real life, as well as on TV. The boys' lives were so profoundly insane, they could not have known what they were doing when they killed tiny James.

Finding, charging, and punishing the boys was not part of any act of forgiveness, rather the opposite. Justice systems all over the world are simply our best effort given our perceptual restriction; but in reality they are managed by the liar also. We should be very clear that there is no way these tiny, inexperienced minds, polluted with abuse, fear, and neglect, could have possibly known what they were doing with any sense of reason. Even so, we prefer to consider the two boys as inherently *evil*, worse than us, two of the unlucky few who - randomly, it seems - get a larger share of the evilness dealt out to every human being at birth.

The only thing we believe these sorts deserve is destruction of their bodies; except the justice system had already outlawed execution in the UK so that was not possible, and we had stopped hanging children an even longer time ago. Nevertheless, execution is the only thing that pleases the liar-mind. The fact that these two are still alive and kicking, and we have extended no forgiveness to them in any sense at all, is why the insanity keeps rearing its ugly head. Furthermore, although perceptually we have consigned the boys' souls to an eternity of hell from which there is no escape, bizarrely we are not satisfied even with that and still want to destroy their bodies, and those of anyone connected with them too. Be clear that this is the liar, promoting the body as our one true identity, to kill with or be killed by, to attack with or be attacked by. Be clear also that this is the very same voice that instructed two small boys to end three lives that day in 1993.

Imagine yourself a tiny child with an alcoholic mother who could hardly do anything for you and five older brothers that beat you up incessantly, took you out on stealing sprees, and sexually abused you. Your parents had both experienced much the same as this in their own lives, so no-one close to you knew anything different. You accepted this life as normal, and discovered innovative and rather clever ways to survive your horrendous experiences. Imagine never experiencing any care or love from your parents at all as they were either too busy with your profoundly sick siblings or their own turbulent relationships issues. Imagine being so sensitive that any word against you sent you into a violent and uncontrollable rage. You might develop tendencies to attract attention that were, in truth, misguided attempts to find some love, any love at all. But what love could you find in environments like these? There would only be fearfulness; day after day of terror, tears, and abuse. Imagine, too, you meet someone just like yourself, someone who is suffering the same hell as you are, someone suffering incessant bullying and abuse, someone who has no role model with any positive impact at all. You might feel relief as your new ally salves the bitter sting of isolation. You might forge a strong partnership; us against the world, it might seem.

The liar is behind this hardship and suffering, and nothing and no-one else is to blame. The liar promotes and publicises the human requirement for pain and misery, while we go along with it. We seek comfort in alcohol, drugs, and other distracting activities to avoid looking at the hellish situations we have made for ourselves; and so we are never able to fix our lives, ending them in the same pain and fear in which they started. We know something big is missing; we are just never sure what it is. Most often, we mistake it for that which will hurt us even more. Along the road, we find others like us who we are mistakenly sure will help us and make us whole again. We reckon that joining forces with a special other is the solution to our pain, so we form relationships that will never last and will always reflect and intensify the destructiveness in our own minds - even when these relationships are relatively comfortable and seemingly peaceful.

Our children learn from us, whoever we are and whatever we say and do - or not say and do - and if we are intensely destructive in our thinking our children will become intensely destructive too. If we endure and exhibit extreme levels of self-loathing, our children will take that on too. If violence is a daily norm, violence will be acceptable in the lives of our children. If unhealthy sexual activity is reasonable, our children will pick that up and re-enact it in their own pained relationships. We are responsible for our children; for their every thought and their every experience. If we ignore and neglect them we can expect an equal measure of self-neglect in their lives also. When they grow up and mess up, we must carry some of the responsibility.

Moreover, culturally, we are *all* responsible for the children, and if we have violent, criminal, and sexually explicit films, books, and media in the environment, our children will pick that up and replicate it somehow. This is our world and we are all complicit in the disaster of it in some way. It is not so difficult to see and we are all aware of it one way or another. Denying the facts simply protects the liar in the mind while the unrelenting guilt arising from such collective complicity is what is truly behind the desire for vengeance, the howling for blood, and the intensity of such feelings. Furthermore, because we are all connected, we feel the guilt very keenly, projecting our own personal responsibility for the death and corruption of innocents onto anyone and anything we can.

When two little boys decide that kidnapping a baby is a good idea, we can be sure that their minds are so out of balance that the liar is screaming inside them, egging them on to more severe levels of violence and, hopefully, to eventually a real body killing. There will be a better-than, worse-than element to this inner voice's caterwauling, as each boy attempts to outdo the other. The lack of good sense that might stop them continuing with their mad scheme is due to levels of fearfulness and life experiences, and not to some inherent *badness* or *evilness* that singles them out as different from the rest of us.

Whatever fear had already been experienced by Robert and Jon, and whatever extra fear was inspired by their meeting, was given expression in the brutal murder of the innocent two-year-old James. This desperate act was the result of two small children defending themselves, in whatever way they could, against the horrendous lives they were enduring. Thoughts that may have crossed their minds that afternoon, fuelling the madness onward, could have been the importance of maintaining the friendship, the human connection that was like no other they had ever known. They may have been seduced into keeping the liar happy by doing, or avoiding doing, something they believed the other wanted or didn't want. They may have felt the need to avoid put downs and *losing face* by not going along with the plan. The crime itself was undoubtedly a projection of what they unconsciously felt should be happening to their own bodies, and what they did to James was no different than that which they were watching in horror films on a regular basis. They even tried to bring James back to life with a battery, like one of their toys. They were not sure if James was real or not.

We must be certain that we would all - yes *all* of us - have done the same thing, in the same shoes, and having had the same life experience as Jon and Robert that cruel afternoon decades ago. This was a dark day in England indeed, but if you think you would not have done the same thing as they, given the same circumstances, you have misunderstood everything we have said about the liar in the mind, and you believe that you are better than other human beings. This is madness, it simply cannot be true. We are all the same. There is only one species and we share everything within it; the good as well as the bad. The forms our lives take appear unlimited in their differences, but not so far underneath appearances we are the same; one equal consciousness, doing the best we can with the limited options available to us; destruction or more intense destruction.

This particular example of the apparently *unforgivable* is not just a case of struggling to forgive an appalling murder. This is the liar's greatest achievement, its field day, because it has managed to persuade us to condemn the truly innocent, the children, the minds that we ourselves are responsible for forming. This is a big win for the liar. If we believe that children can be *evil* then the liar has succeeded in its goal. If children are *evil*, then separateness must be true because there can be no real interconnectedness between humans. If children are condemnable, then *evil* and *badness* are real, external, and indisputable, and we have no power over anything at all. We are assuredly lost as a species if our children can be *evil*. Yet only humans suffer this madness, and not all humans. If we notice the irrationality of this idea, we might also notice our arrogance and insane belief in our false better-than-ness.

If we find the process of forgiving anyone to be difficult, and if we find the notion of forgiveness as presenting us with endless and continuous opportunities, then it is likely we have misunderstood the liar's functioning. True forgiveness is a side-effect of understanding the liar in the mind and needs no extra effort. When we recognise the liar and see its intentions clearly, we have no option but to forgive every living soul that exists, or has ever existed, for anything they might have done.

There is no effort in this either. We do not have to work at forgiveness. There is simply no other way of thinking about all life other than that it is, at the root, and behind the dark and illusory filter of destruction, wholly innocent. The problems we have, and our abhorrent behaviour, are due to believing the liar's voice is our own, and this is the only problem we have.

The liar is just an evolutionary stepping stone, bridging deep, ancient, animal-like levels of fearfulness towards a fearless, joyous, and peaceful humanity. The liar's whims may appear intricate and complicated but, in truth, they are meaningless and always about maintaining fear and separation. Inventing the liar in the mind to protect ourselves is the only, and inevitable, thing we could have done with our new awareness and language when we received them, given that we did not know our own minds at the time and had been in the grip of fear ever since we could remember. However, now, finally, we are beginning to see.

If forgiveness is difficult then there are some ideas the liar tells us we want to cherish still, even though they are lies and so must be destructive in some sense. We might want to protect our right to define ourselves with violent and aggressive labels. We might want to protect our right to own things or people and enjoy worldly power. We might want to maintain our obsession with how our body appears. We are welcome to protect and so keep these things if we wish but, by doing so, we are only allowing the liar to remain in control of our minds. We may have eliminated a little bit of false thinking here and there but if any part of the liar's theology remains, and if the tiniest bit of the liar's world is reasonable, forgiveness will feel like a great struggle and finding our way out of hell will seem an impossible task.

When we forgive, it must be total if it is to be effective. We cannot half-forgive a person without maintaining the world as it is. There can be no half-forgiveness because one act of forgiveness is like any other. When I can truly forgive my best friend his petty meanness, I have forgiven Hitler at the same time. This is the nature of forgiveness; it extends to all in an instant. This is also why we must understand what leads us to acts which give rise to the need for forgiveness. Suffering and fearfulness cause us to act regrettably in order to attempt to alleviate the pain we are enduring. Eventually, we must see all acts needing forgiveness as desperate attempts to escape fearfulness, instead of coming from the existence of an external *evilness*. In the end, it will become apparent that any defence (and thus attack) is raised on the liar's behalf alone. First, we need to see how that is so; then *evil*, *badness*, and the liar itself cannot retain any authenticity.

Humanity is one species. Like the leaves on a tree, we share our collective experience and little separates us in reality. However, the liar has us believe that there is no tree uniting us; that instead we are all alone, separate beings, isolated and fearful, pitted against the others, entirely different and unique. This is not true at all, but as long as we believe it, the world will continue to be as it is. We will be able to justify war, murder, violence, and vengeance. If we are able to see what we share, the bad as well as the good, we may feel compassion instead of rage about those people we previously condemned to hell.

If one leaf on the tree of humanity is as important as all the others, we will feel love and compassion for the murderers, the rapists, the paedophiles, and the polluters. From love comes healing. If only some leaves are important, we will cyclically move towards devastation with the conflict and hatred that must ensue from such a belief in inequality. If no leaf is important, the liar wins; an impossible situation in truth. As one act of forgiveness is just the same as any other, one human is, in truth, no better or worse than any other. We are all just dealing with the life experiences we have been handed as best we can, even when we believe that nothing and no-one is important.

The British press also had a field day with the murder of James Bulger, as you might imagine they would. The media operates at the liar's behest, where potentially important news is deemed insignificant when compared to who a celebrity slept with, or which celebrity did something appalling, or anything that incites rage and bloodthirstiness in the population, such as can be counted on with the Bulger case, which still sells a great many newspapers whenever something new happens.

The liar told us that these two little boys should be condemned for all eternity, branded *evil*, never to be saved; and the press echoed its voice. We were angry, we were raging, and we wanted blood. We got as close to it as we could in that the courts of England tried these two little boys as adults. They were sent to jail and we all got our pound of flesh, but it did not satisfy as we are still raging, and families are still in hiding, and the lawyers for the boys are still receiving death threats. We openly, yet unconsciously, demonstrate our collective guilt for constructing and supporting the foundations of this nightmare world; the liar's world that has resulted in countless and inevitable horrors for which we dare not accept responsibility. Yet, at some level of consciousness, we all know the truth and we cannot keep it hidden.

Since then, this horrific story regularly comes up for re-examination in the UK because we did not heal our minds through vengeance, as we never will. Vengeance and punishment will never bring us peace. One of the lads broke his parole recently by having looked at child pornography. The other fares better by all accounts. However, whatever goes on, no healing has occurred in the national psyche and true forgiveness evades us.

Love is love. It does not change. It does not condone or support destructive actions. But it does not betray the doer of destructive actions either, regardless of what they have done. Love is unconditional and is not saved for those who don't murder innocent babies. The only way we can solve the riddle and the pain of our world is by extending love to all.

Little James Bulger is our human brother and it is heart breaking that he was killed in such a way. It is also heart-breaking that the human mind under the liar's control supports a world in which killings like this are reasonable, tiringly witnessed daily on the media, and yet horrifically inexplicable when they happen close by. If it is dark-skinned children, half-a-world away, being hacked-to-death in their thousands by other children, we are not so bothered about that. However, one of our own, an event that might bring down our own self-proclaimed better-than-ness, this must be solid proof of *evil* in our midst.

James Bulger was an innocent and, as we have seen, the liar must destroy innocence. For the other two innocents, Robert and Jon, the fact that their minds had already been seduced by the liar to such an extreme degree meant that the destruction of the innocent, the representative of that which they believed they were not - even at such a young age - promised them an escape from the pain of the madness they were enduring. In the same way we wantonly killed the Christ that afternoon 2000 years ago, these boys did the unthinkable. And they were not relieved of their fearfulness either, as neither were we, contrary to assurances. The promises of the liar are never kept and we have never found peace by doing its bidding.

If we can forgive Robert Thompson and Jon Venables by understanding that there is *no way* they could have known what they were doing when they killed little James Bulger, then we are free. As long as we fail to see that the liar is in control of every human mind, these events will continue, ceaseless, in varying grotesque forms; until perhaps we destroy ourselves and there are no more humans around to behave appallingly, and no-one to gossip or buy newspapers about it either.

I'm sad we live in a world in which children murder children. However, I hope to help show that there is a way out of this world of pain, and I have strong and reliable assurances that we can leave this nightmare behind. When we see the liar in our minds, noticing its full potential, we cannot help but realise that all the horrors of which we despair have been inevitable. Furthermore, if I can pass over a vile thought not my own, I can pass over all destructive thoughts I ever have; being sure that the vilest of them is as meaningless as the petty, bitter, complaining, worse-than and better-than ideas. This is what we must do with the majority of our thoughts, because they are not our own. Let us begin to see that all thinking that does not come from a foundation of love is untrue.

James did not live a valueless life if he can help us find our way to true forgiveness, to healing our minds, and to building a world in which we would be happy to let our children grow up. How any of us can justify bringing more humans into the world as it is right now is astonishing; but we have been lulled into sleep by the liar. We fail to notice neither our own destructive tendencies nor how we have accepted a nightmare for a reasonable way of life. Yet the door of true forgiveness, of freedom, is now open. Let us walk through, hand in hand; you and I, James, Robert, Jon, and all humanity. Let us be healed, softly and quietly. Let us wake up together from this vicious, hostile dream and finally save the world.

5 ONLINE BULLIES AND SEXUAL PREDATORS

Before we can free ourselves from the liar, we must understand what it is exactly we are freeing ourselves from. If we do not look at the liar and its activities very closely, how can we hope to know what it is or understand our difficult life experiences, or those of anyone else?

Enjoying a Saturday afternoon public execution was a normal pastime for centuries - and still is in some places. While we remain unaware of the problem, we might continue to indulge it erroneously. If we remain ignorant of the dictatorship of our minds, we may miss undoing a false idea that continues to cause much suffering in the world. If we cannot look, carefully and dispassionately, at all our thoughts and beliefs, we are likely to save for ourselves an *evil* deed for which we will be damned for all eternity.

Forgiveness is not saying, *OK, so you did this bad thing, and you recompensed somehow, but we will always remember that you did this bad thing*. This is not forgiveness because this ensures sin is real, existing forever. This cannot be right, and isn't, thank goodness. Instead, forgiveness comes from the realisation that we know not what we do. In fact, we have no idea what we are doing or why we are doing it because we are not listening to our own true voice. Instead, we listen to and believe lies, and act from these mistaken beliefs alone. Yet, thankfully, no-one has to believe a lie eternally.

We usually find sex crimes rather appalling. It wasn't always so, and in some cultures even today they remain ignored and hidden, as if they were no concern to people from *these* better-than cultures. Whenever they do spill out into the public eye, spoiling our overinflated view of ourselves, we label a great many of them *unforgivable*. However, these crimes share a similar form to what many consider acceptable in the world. Violence in relationships, however subtle, is violence. Sexual objectification of a person in a relationship (a belief in the ownership of their body), however subtle, strips them of their independence, autonomy, and rights. Interestingly, it is with sex crimes primarily that we shift guilt onto the victim with the least difficulty. There is a reason for this - liar-based of course - but I'm not going to tackle it until later on.

Sadly, we are not even close to thinking healthily about sex. Even if we have managed to convince ourselves that foolish giggling and lewd remarking about the opposite gender's body parts is reasonable, or pornography is reasonable, or a long series of sexual partners is reasonable, these are just exercises in avoiding the truth. We believe our behaviour is normal, failing to notice we haven't advanced much from the higher primates. Aside from gender role confusion, we haven't discarded any of the beliefs that we brought into humanness from lower evolutionary states. We continue to believe that *he* who fucks the most is the winner, and that *she* should be owned by a *he*, and be fucked by *him* whenever *he* likes.

In fact, human sexual behaviour is much more destructive than that of our nearest evolutionary neighbours - and not because we add to *fucking the most, and hardest*, bringing in the required element of violence and aggression reserved for males. Animals just do it, with plain and simple references to worse-than and better-than states; communities of primates just getting on with it, with the odd usurpation and revolt from a male attempting to experience being the best for a while, and why wouldn't you if you were a terrified and isolated male chimpanzee? As humans, sex is defined by all these primal beliefs and behaviour patterns that we inherited from our simian ancestry, without yet seeing that we did. Then, on top of all that, we add our psychological hang ups, separation psychosis, language inventions, stories and fantasies, better and worse preoccupations, and all the perceptual mess that makes us, currently, what the human race is.

Sex is just sex, but humans do it for a million other reasons aside from its purpose, procreation. We do it to elevate our status, to perpetually relieve ourselves (apparently), to avoid being alone, to feed our children, to pay for our drug habits, to relieve an addiction, to reset the balance of our lives, to please our partner, to assure ourselves of our better-ness or worseness, to show off to our friends, and to control and bully others, amongst other reasons. Moreover, because we are so fearful in every area of our lives, sex becomes another arena for the projection of this fearfulness. We attack and defend each other and ourselves, using sex as our weapon of choice.

Human sex requires a special relationship in which two people believe they have found salvation in each other. Any relationship that is based upon overpowering another, particularly through sex, is an insane relationship which promises peace to both parties but leads them further into chaos at every step. Such relationships may last just a second in time, or perhaps a whole lifetime, with little real difference in content. In these sorts of relationships, we play out our fear and loathing with each other, the same echoes of despair coming from a quiet sixty-year-old marriage and a violent rape.

We are all deeply fearful and we are all doing our best to find relief from this fearfulness. The fact that, mostly, we do not realise this means the liar has full control. All the opportunities that come our way, promising us a little peace, are liar orchestrated, and so inevitably lead us into more pain. Occasionally, we lose our minds so spectacularly we act outrageously, causing suffering to ourselves and others. However, in the moment we do these unpleasant things, we believe they are justified. This is because a little voice we think is our own advocates the detrimental course of action in mantra-form, promising that by going along with it we will undoubtedly experience a better-than state, as well as peace; promises never kept.

The liar uses anything it can get its grubby little hands on that might serve its dastardly purposes. Neuro-linguistic programming, or NLP, is a recent arrival to the science of mind and a useful one at that. We have discovered that we can re-train our minds into thinking positively by affirmation practices, such as those suggested by Louise Hay and others, and so heal our lives. It is a very powerful and efficacious process, the results of which are undeniable. Nevertheless, as you know, I'm not here to tell you about the good stuff we do. I'll get to that eventually, but right now I have trickier work. I'm here to tell you that all the *bad* stuff we do isn't *bad* at all.

Any psychological practice that can alter reality to how we might prefer it is most definitely going to interest the liar and, due to the undeniable power of NLP over the human mind, it is no surprise it has found its way into the wrong hands. Like the wicked hypnotists who fool unsuspecting folk into eating raw onions in front of their friends, the wrong hands we are discussing here belong to those finding the fear of human existence overwhelming. The liar in the mind persuades us that we will assuredly find relief from fear, pain, and suffering by gaining control over the minds of those we believe have hurt us.

Sexual predators, desiring to control the minds of their prey, are predominantly men. This is not surprising because, if we describe ourselves with overwhelmingly violent and aggressive labels, such as those reserved for the masculine, we are far more likely to experience extreme levels of fearfulness; the levels of fear required for propelling us into harmful activities. The liar has split us perceptually down the middle in terms of gender and we all agree with the roles it gives us. Men get a bagful of violent, aggressive, and fearful adjectives to describe themselves with their whole lives, while women get the opposite, rather peaceful and loving adjectives. These descriptive labels are set at birth. We do not get to choose whether to accept them or not; accept them we must. We could say that, in most cases, the feminine labels get proved immediately by our loving mothers, without whom we would not be here; our very first idea. The counterpart labels of isolation, fear, and aggression do not receive a similarly immediate validation, so the liar must support the fear and denigrate the love, which it gets started on immediately.

All this goes towards explaining the boisterous behaviour of little boys and the quiet, anxious nature of little girls. We understand and accept our false roles from very early on. There is nothing at all random about it and it is indeed a travesty. Never mind pink or blue clothes, these labelling ideas are stuck like superglue in the mind, never questioned, always accepted, our crazy world arising from them.

We define strength as physical dominance in the world governed by the liar. Men, in general, have more physical strength than women. However, if men were truly the strongest, by definition, then that would be that, end of story. However, the definition is spurious; the real meaning warped by the liar into serving its own ends. Thus, the lie needs constant defence because it is not true.

This erroneous definition of *strength* we all agree upon, must defend itself, protect itself, and remain constantly on the uneasy alert. If we are strong, in truth, how could we be fearful at the same time? What we define as strength is surely not strength at all if it can never be safe. Physical dominance as a definition of strength is a lie covering deep vulnerability and fragility. It is a glaring lie we have believed for far too long. The liar offers deeply fearful men the possibility of relieving themselves of the fear they inherited at birth without choice by physically overpowering others. When it comes to the arena of sex, the victim is usually female - the weaker sex; weakness being defined by lack of physical strength primarily, but having spilt over into many other perceptual areas of life, as is plain to see.

Nowadays, the Internet - as a projection of the collective mind space - offers the fearful a dull curtain to hide behind. Anonymity is available to those who have not yet become insane to the degree of being able to outwardly reveal their abusive thought patterns. Shadowy NLP practices, used by sexual predators and pubescent boys, are now all over the Internet and elsewhere, and the only reason why this is so is due to the profound fearfulness of men suffering dire misconceptions about themselves.

Let's educate ourselves a little bit. What are NLP seduction techniques? Well, why not just google *NLP seduction* and you'll get a good idea about what some men think is a valuable way to spend their time. Among a fair amount of vileness, I see women compared to Pavlov dogs; say the right thing and they'll be begging you for sex, apparently. When you are done, you'll find similar techniques to eliminate them from your personal lives with ease. There's even a wiki page! It's mainstream reasonableness. This is a very unpleasant business indeed. These are men who have no concern about the autonomy of a female, or the personhood of a female; and this is exactly how the higher primates, and indeed most of the animal world functions.

There is something very wonderful about human consciousness and what it can achieve, but ignoring our gifts and remaining in the swamp is also a choice open to us. Lack of concern for other people's rights and autonomy means a lack of concern for our own autonomy, because what we see outside is a reflection of how we treat ourselves and what is happening inside our own minds. This better-than state of mind is very stuck, very unhappy. It attempts to win a bizarre competition through these unpleasant activities, but it never achieves its goal. Instead, like the junkie's next fix, a desperate need arises for more of this illusory power that, like strength misinterpreted, cannot uphold its own definition. The need gets greater and greater because, as with drugs, the drug itself is not the answer to the problem. We must ask ourselves where the trail might end for some of these guys. They are very sick brothers, so what can we do?

Firstly, we can imagine what may have caused the intense levels of fearfulness required to provoke such deplorable actions. We can imagine early experiences of abuse at the hands of women. We can imagine the put-downs, scathing words, manipulation, and more abuse coming from the females they have admired as they got older. We can imagine the severe personal pain ensuing as yet another attempt at connecting with a woman fails spectacularly. We can imagine this suffering becoming very intense, particularly when exacerbated by some sort of perceived physical inadequacy. We can imagine an education coming from culture and those around them about the worthlessness of women. We can imagine ourselves being seduced into attempting to reset the balance of power in exactly the same way. We should be able to easily relate all of this to an abuse of power we ourselves have committed.

The truth is there is not one of us who would not do the same thing under the same circumstances. Furthermore, the truth is that the only thing these people are asking for - our human family members - is help and understanding; even when they believe themselves to be enjoying the temporary and vacuous pleasures of overpowering someone they have evaluated, superficially, as weaker than they. When we are clear minded, we see that their victim must be someone they consider more powerful, given the need to twist them into powerlessness by misuse of NLP practices. A bully is always full of fear and always needs our help, let's never forget it.

When we understand what is in the mind of our brother we cannot hate him or be angry with him anymore. We must remain sad, however, while he is hurting and lashing out in order to try and protect himself from his own fearfulness. Although the distressing actions continue and we will never condone them, our compassion for our brothers will reach out into the world and touch hearts closed to love and gentleness for eons. This is the true work of forgiveness.

Forgiveness is a by-product of understanding what the liar is. Once we know about the liar in our minds, and how it has built this grotesque illusion of a world we believe is real, we see that things could only be as they are, at this moment. All regrettable acts come about from the belief in lies alone. How can we blame or condemn when we know that we have all been hypnotised by the liar into believing that separation and destruction is our only worthy goal, all behaviour following from this simple mistaken belief. Our brother, believing he is powerful by successfully tricking women into having sex with him, and so briefly experiencing the status of winner in the tribe, simply emulates that which controls us all. The fact that he cannot be true to himself gnaws away at his soul. The road in which his fearfulness takes him is the bitter road of damnation, the road on which we all walk.

When we are fearful, we are desperate for help and love. When we were tiny and became fearful, mother came with food, warmth, love, and cuddles. As we grew older, mother stopped coming but the fearfulness remained. Thus, we had to develop our own skills in order to deal with the constant fear, independently of mother. Sometimes our fearfulness was very acute and we were so desperate for help that our behaviour, born of this fearfulness, became lamentable.

The liar's one and only function is to separate and it does this by convincing us of our better-ness and worse-ness when compared to others. Ironically, the better-than state is a double lie because it cannot be reached outside of the total annihilation of all life; the liar's totally insane and impossible end-goal. Thus, even when we are sure of our betterness when compared to others, not so far below that is the certainty we are utterly worthless. This is most easily seen in emotions such as arrogance, in which overtly pronounced better-than ideas barely cover the fear and dread. All forms of human separation psychosis are simply varying degrees of unworthiness, always requiring punishment.

The liar in our minds has produced all the fear we have ever known. Believing ourselves to be alone and vulnerable, fear is inevitable. When fear becomes an acceptable part of life, the constant lies we hear telling us we are unworthy, stupid, and hated, become reasonable and accepted; a constant, rarely noticed drone of self-disapproval.

The twisting and turning machinations of the liar can persuade us into acting in extremely unhelpful and destructive ways. But we would never act like this if we hadn't already mistaken these actions as a remedy for our fearfulness, something to redress our unworthiness, the help we so desperately need. And these desperate actions are always suggested by a voice not our own that we have trusted in error. They are not our true ideas. Underneath the aggression, abuse, and violence is the true voice of the innocent one; the real Us. It pleads softly: *Help me. I do not know what I do.* Can anyone be justified in responding with anger to such a plea for help? We may not be aware of this voice. We may have even managed to convince ourselves that what we are doing is beneficial and enjoyable, even when it is wholly destructive. Yet our true voice is never far away.

Sexual predators indulge in power games and believe they are winners. What they do not see is that only an already self-defined loser needs to play such games; and power(less) games, when examined honestly, never deliver their promise or, as with vengeance, the need for them would have disappeared a long time ago. NLP seduction is just another form that fearful bullying has taken recently; a rather modern one. However, bullying is the same whatever form it might take and wherever it dares raise its terrified head. From the violent usurpation of the head-bully in the monkey community in order to take the bullying rights for oneself, to systematically destroying our tiny classmate at school with endless insults, to ecstatically robbing millions of pensioners of their life savings, all bullies are lauded by the rest of us who also believe in all versions of better-than. However, there is never any difference in the content of better-than. Winning, as the liar has it, means the destruction of others.

We believe we are in control of our own minds and the choices we make, and we go about our daily lives as if this were so. However, it is blatantly not the case. We fail to see that we are compelled to act out our fears and complexes within all our relationships, and in all areas of our lives, one way or another. We are unable to see the problem in ourselves and instead think we are in control. We constantly look outside to watch everyone careening haphazardly through their lives, buffeted around at the whim of the liar. We point, judge, and recriminate. *We are not like them*, we assure ourselves, as we crash into similar pain and suffering.

In 2012, an innocent sister of ours, Amanda Todd, committed suicide because she had been bullied incessantly by an innocent brother of ours who had found comfort from fear in attacking those he felt weaker than himself. This is not an isolated case and, sadly, more suicides of young people have taken place recently due to online bullying. The cyberbully is just another projection of the liar into worldly form. It has done a very good job here, as it always does. It uses the anonymity of the Internet to provide a hiding place from which it can express itself in ways it was not able to before.

Previously, we kept destructive behaviour born of the hatred of others at bay due to another very strong liar principle of not doing anything that might make us look bad in the eyes of others. Nowadays, the Internet has given us the opportunity to ignore that particular lie of not losing face and we are able to express ourselves in any manner we like, safe in the knowledge that it is highly unlikely we will be caught, or our regular lives put in jeopardy. Young people living in this virtual reality, usually still at school, find themselves ruled by a set of moral values that would leave the majority of the adult world in total chaos. These values are to do with being the meanest and nastiest, where better-than is the most fearful, the scariest, they who care the least about the others. The liar will express itself in any format and we are now providing it with environments in which it can wreak the most havoc, at its behest no doubt.

Who knows what the online bully is going through? Undoubtedly it is extremely painful. Whatever suffering they have endured, or are enduring, we cannot know; but we can be sure that they are suffering. What we do know is that the liar will have told them that freedom from fear comes from powerfulness, and that powerfulness comes from the destruction of others. They will have believed this lie and acted upon it. The false power that they seek is born of a deep sense of their own personal weakness, another lie. Yet this lie has been repeatedly proven by life experiences that have informed them, time and time again, that they are worthless, no-good, worse-than, and deserve punishment. Living with a state of mind like this is intolerable so, misguided, they seek to redress their perceived powerlessness in the only way they think they can; by destroying those they believe have caused them pain.

That they are never relieved of their fear does not deter them, nor cause them to question their activities. In fact, the rush they experience at each petty win over their chosen *victim* ensures their addiction to such cruelty in the chase for these temporary and meaningless triumphs. They do not know what they do because they do not know why they do it. Furthermore, they do not know why they do it because they have no idea about the existence of the liar in their minds or that this perceptual virus is running their lives.

On the other hand, we must look at our innocent sister, the so-called *victim*, and ask ourselves what sort of lies she must have believed that caused such a devastating relationship to unfold. Who knows what the *prey* is going through? Whatever it is we can be sure it is extremely painful. Whatever it is we can be sure it is born of deep fear coming from a personal belief in worthlessness and lack of love in her life, a desperate need for help. When someone offered her the freedom from fear which she was desperately seeking, as we all are in some form, she had very little choice but to accept. It was the only reasonable option provided.

What is the real difference between the *predator* and the *prey*? The truth is, none. No-one in the same place, predator or prey, would have acted any differently under the same circumstances. This is what we need to understand and is the key to freeing our minds from the liar. Only the liar causes these sad events in our beautiful, abundant, and innocent world.

When we miss the desperate call for assistance in any fearful act our sleeping fellows perform, how can we change the world? If a mind is in torment then we, as a unified humanity, are in torment. The help we must give is understanding and compassion. When we understand that, up until now, it has only been possible to not know what we have been doing or why, we are able to shine away the dark shadows that were previously set up as harsh realities by our minds under dictatorship.

When we understand that there is no over there, no external, nothing worse than us, and that anything that appals us, causing us to condemn, will have its hiding place in our own hearts, we will be able to begin the undoing of the liar in the collective consciousness. By bringing our light to the dark shadows of human suffering, we will reveal the shadows to be nothing at all, just mistakes arising from pathological ignorance. We will deny anything that goes against our true dignity, innocence, and eternal beauty; that which is *All* that we are.

6 DELHI GANG-RAPE-MURDER

We should try to understand rape, from a peaceful and non-condemning point of view, as the human-identified-as-masculine's attempt to project his fear and guilt, and so rid himself of it, onto the label by which he is not defined, his opposite, the *them* to his *us*, the worse-than to his better-than, the feminine. There is no other reason for gender abuse of this form, although the liar will be delighted to persuade us there is and, by doing so, obfuscate the truth and avoid being uncovered as the main culprit.

Gender abuse is the liar's game at its most effective. Only men rape, or use their bodies as weapons in this sense. Instances of women accused of rape or sexual abuse remain exceptional; outside the sadly commonplace situation of overwhelming levels of sexual attack and defence activity coming from the masculine, across the world.

We inherited the belief that the masculine winner is entitled to own females from our nearest evolutionary cousins. However, human consciousness cannot avoid awareness of the fact that the ownership of another equal human being is impossible, and thus any attempt to do so invokes inevitable guilt.

We might hear about rare instances of sexual abuse at the hands of women as if they were significant, but they are usually brought up by the liar to divert attention. It does remain to be said, however, that the liar does not care who is more powerful in its illusory and iniquitous world, as long as inequality and conflict remain. Currently, women shoulder the underling *victim* label, but a thousand years from now, if we fail to eradicate the liar from our minds, this could easily be upside-down. Whoever the *winner* might be is an arbitrary matter from the liar's perspective, as long as the *winner* is the one who can cause the most destruction at a particular point in time. Given that, currently, we have physical strength as the measure of power and dominance, the masculine must be the *winner* when we are taking sides, which we usually are.

In the present epoch, the unconscious masculine feels entitled to women, to the ownership of a woman, or women. This is an evolutionary hangover coming from our older, simian mind. We haven't advanced very far in an evolutionary sense and it is not all that long ago in the West when women held no human rights at all, outside of the protection of their husbands. Even today, perceptually, men do the choosing (asking) of who they want to marry, while women wait to be chosen.

We should not forget, of course, that the underlings in any oppressive situation will naturally become resourceful, as we should expect. Sadly, we use this fact for blame-shifting in the gender war, even today in the apparently advanced Western mind. That the oppressed are manipulative, scheming, and therefore *evil* and condemnable are ideas we used to commonly hear from the mouths of racists insisting on the non-human status of their chosen non-human. Nowadays, we consider idea like these unacceptable, except from within the gender arena. This is an interesting anomaly and worth looking at in more depth.

If you were a woman around a century ago in the West you were basically chattel by law. Today, in some cultures, women's status has not budged much from being an item in of a man's inventory and, even in the West, the idea of the ownership of women runs deep. The lie that women need a man to look after them, to provide for them and the children, is deeply engrained, very powerful, and difficult to discard. Recent attempts made by women to break free from these perceptual chains have mistakenly assumed that taking on the aggressive, competitive behaviour, and fearful, self-identifying labels of men is the way to freedom, to the detriment of all.

In the same way that we who believe we never have enough financially feel divinely entitled to that which other people possess and begrudge them it, so does the human mind in a male body believe himself entitled to the ownership of female bodies, becoming resentful when unable to take up such ownership. On the female side, survival requires a male overlord for her body and so how the body appears takes on huge importance, as a good landlord - i.e. one with lots to supply - will not be interested in a poor quality female body as part of the deal. This ownership/owned dichotomy is played out subtly in personal relationships; it explains the fashion and beauty industries; it explains the masculine's addiction to pornography, where paid for images of female bodies suffice as surrogate ownership; it explains the oldest profession in the world; and it also explains rape and sexual abuse.

The liar uses whatever seems to differentiate us to convince us we are alone, separate, and very vulnerable. Our bodies do appear to distinguish us from each other and the liar uses these obvious differences in order to promote superiority or inferiority, whichever idea is more useful to it at the time. Genitalia clearly separate the male from the female, and the liar has had little trouble convincing us to condemn each other dependent on which we were born with. At intensity, these perceived inferiorities are expressed through the hatred and defilement of one body-type by its counterpart, in the form of rape and sexual abuse at one extreme and lewd, disrespectful language and jokes at the other. No-one has missed out on this story becoming indisputable dogma in the mind. Even when we think we disagree with it, we will have saved some of this story for ourselves, somewhere in our perception.

From the roving hand on a crowded train to callous gang rape, none of us, men or women, have escaped the suffering imposed by the belief in the lie of superiority and inferiority based on gender; that which allows the superior to attack and destroy, verbally, physically, and psychologically, with impunity. When victims attempt to speak up, to vent their pain, no-one listens because no one is prepared to even glance at the truth, let alone to accept it. These voices that make us angry, defensive, and indignant, voices which we are compelled to shout down and silence, are the voices of our daughters, our sisters, our mothers, and all our female relatives and friends, and some of our male relatives and friends too. There is no support or help offered because perceptually the world agrees, at some level, that the victim must have deserved this treatment; it was their fault. The young woman who died after a horrific and violent gang-rape on a public bus in Delhi, reportedly apologised to her parents from her death bed. This is what we are dealing with here. When the victim of murder by rape feels she must say sorry.

We can, perhaps, explain the un-evolved and instinctive urges of the animal kingdom by the unconscious drive to procreate. This is not why men rape, however. It is not about sex at all. It is instead about power and fear, about asserting a very fragile belief in superiority and, in masculine terms, doing it through physical dominance and conquest with the use of the defining body part. In war the women are captured and raped, this is the entitlement of the victors. In relationships, a man decides he will have a particular woman and he pushes his way in to her life, while women obsess continually about which man will attempt to push his way in.

In our forgiveness practice we report on the events that make us tearful and sad; a group witnessing of the regrettable things that are occurring, constantly, in our beautiful world. We do not become angry, reactionary, and irrational. The sleeping human mind hears the word *rape*, takes a sharp intake of breath, and hopes it will go away. This is because we are so confused about why we do it. However, by ignoring it, not only do we OK it in some sense, we also agree that the *victim* is guilty in the place of the *aggressor*. We insist victims should keep quiet and certainly not disturb us from our better-than dreaming.

We protect rape and sexual abuse by not looking at it or trying to understand it. We maintain the suffering of our brothers and sisters by assuming sexual abuse is someone else's problem. If we blame the victim, the problem is solved somewhat; embarrassing voices are silenced and we can go back to normal again; back to our quiet, small, anxious little lives. Men may continue to feel justified in their entitlement to women, and the world can continue to spin out of control. We might even be able to avoid looking at our own female relatives' and friends' painful experiences in the world, blaming them somehow, in the hope that we may keep our eyes tightly shut and not have to deal with this tricky business ourselves. Yet all we are doing is proving the liar's key tenet, that guilt can be projected successfully onto victims and so they *must* have deserved such treatment. This is, of course, unutterably insane but is where we all remain, even in the *apparently* liberated West.

Peaceful eradication of gender abuse is perhaps the key to resolving all differences everywhere, because this is the liar's strongest hold over our collective perception. Due to that, it will undoubtedly fight tooth and nail to keep the gender inequality lie intact. We have a lot of work to do here and we should probably start by shifting the focus of healing from the victim to the aggressor and so move closer to the source of the problem and its inevitable solution.

To make a start on forgiving hugely emotive events such as the recent Delhi gang-rape and murder of a young medical student just starting out in life, we must put our own perception inside the mind of the rapists and try to compassionately understand how any human being, including ourselves, could act so destructively. We must do our best in this practice, as it serves to free our own minds from the torment of condemning our brothers. Successful compassionate thinking puts us in the position of being able to resolve conflict in any other situation too.

It appears difficult to say why the notorious gang rape and murder that took place in Delhi in late 2012 provoked such a massive reaction from the populace. However, such group reactions are, as we have seen, the projection of the collective guilt in which we all share. Gender abuse and gang rape is not uncommon in India; Western female tourists, even married ones, suffering it on a regular basis also. In reality, India is not a great place to be female; although Indian females may well disagree with that, even the most oppressed, because the liar does not lie to just one half of us. The Delhi gang-rape-murder showed that people simply had had enough, or perhaps there was some other element at work, such as a caste issue. Whatever may have caused such rage in the populace around this singular, horrific event, it was immediately business-as-usual for the rapists in India, and remains so.

It is clear that there is no real solution in angry reaction, vengeance, or punishment. Again, we are simply projecting our collective guilt arising from supporting a world in which rape and murder are commonplace, as well as encouraging it through our own thinking, even though we are not consciously aware of doing so. The gender lie has made no real shift towards being undone and the forms it takes these days may even be more intense in their application than they used to be. In the West, where women are now more able to stand up to male bullies, we see a concomitant rise in sex crimes against children. What we must do is ask ourselves what state of mind has become so fearful, so powerless, that such behaviour becomes reasonable?

The answer is, first and foremost, that such a mind believes it is a body, unquestioningly labelled with masculine ideas of power and dominance. Words describing masculinity are, invariably, fearful in content. When the masculine is physically symbolised by the penis, and to this physical description is added these violent and aggressive labels, it is not too difficult to see how the penis can be confused with weaponry. It is true that all of us have already taken on these ideas at some level, but what causes some minds to act on these false principles to extremes?

We are talking about minds which have experienced extreme oppression by other similarly labelled mind/body conglomerates; human males who have suffered humiliation, poverty, even violence and aggression from their own side; minds that cannot support their own feelings of inferiority in the eyes of others while hearing a daily cultural mantra that the female is *weaker, worse-than, worthless*. There is no doubt that intense levels of self-loathing, abuse, and bullying can cause people to seek redress by sharing their pain with another person believed to be weaker. Female persons fall into that category easily, especially in India.

Whatever the reasons behind horrific acts of violence, we know that a person believes and acts upon lies alone: lies based on masculine status defined by the ownership and entitlement of females. These are beliefs handed to us as perceptual *givens*. They come from lower stages of evolution on earth and we accept them without question. They are lies needing defence from any humiliation and degradation in the personal life experience. They are lies based on better-than, worse-than preoccupations, and false advice as to how to alleviate fearfulness. Murderous gang rape is the liar's idea alone. It could have never arisen in the peaceful mind of the noble human beings we truly are.

As the terror commenced, the liar will have been assuring these fearful ones that they would most certainly lose face if they did not go along with the others. The voice of doom suggested to them that if they were *even worse* than the others, they would be the true winner; that by destroying this innocent female body in the sickest way imaginable they would find their way out of their own personal suffering. Reports said she apologised, as if it was her fault. This apology is the key to understanding what rape and abuse based on gender is about, and finding our way out of this perceptual mess.

The belief that we are separate from, and unequal to, each other generates a profound level of fear and guilt, as well as the certainty we are to be condemned and punished at any moment for believing and acting upon what we know, deep down, to be impossible. All humans suffer this complex at varying levels of intensity, even when we are unaware of it and claim to believe something the opposite. The fact is we cannot be separate from each other, so the belief that we are causes a huge split in our minds and, instead of facing the problem as it is, the liar bids us deny it and instead project it into unlimited forms in the world. We never get to see the real issue for all the distraction. This abstract, core form of the separation psychosis we all suffer, is the super-class of all our other fears.

The liar tells us, and we believe, that we can shift our own fearfulness onto another person and by doing so relieve ourselves of our burden of guilt. The other person, or people, we single out for this will be those defined as *weaker than* and *worse than* us. The most obvious and widespread of the dualistic differentiators is gender and, as long as the focus of our compassion remains on the *victims*, as per the liar's design again, we will not get near to solving this problem. We have been dealing entirely with the effects and not the cause, and this is the liar's wish. This needs to change.

So it is all down to believing a lie, feeling guilty for doing so and then attempting to get rid of the guilt by dumping it onto someone else. We all believe it is possible to rid ourselves of guilt in this way. We all believe, too, that we have received guilt not our own and taken it on successfully. Thankfully, all this is impossible, but while we believe it to be true it causes us endless mental suffering with no clear solution to any of it. It is all completely insane and we are all complicit in the madness in some way.

We are not excusing anything here, by the way, but we need to understand why we behave the way we do because, if we don't understand the problem, we are likely to label each other *evil* at the liar's suggestion. Labelling a person *evil* means we are doomed to remain in the fearful hell we have built with our faulty thinking because there is no-one responsible for anything if it can never be ourselves. Pointing the finger means that gender abuse, as well as any other human horror, remains unresolvable. Healing and resolution will never be an option under the liar's instruction.

Vengeance and violent punishment is just a deflection of the real problem again and we quickly find ourselves behaving like those we defined as less than human. Vicious revenge on rapists has done absolutely nothing about gender abuse, which continues unabated. We all have blood on our hands while we perceptually split human beings into *better* and *worse* by gender - or in any way at all - however subtle. The divisive ideas, thoughts, jokes, throw-away comments, and beliefs we all indulge in on a daily basis are the seeds of the horrors we are unable to comprehend.

When we accept the liar as the only enemy, we can see that we all have exactly the same problem. We also see that we would do *exactly* the same thing given the same circumstances as these poor, fearful men who were so tormented in their minds that destroying the innocent was seen as the only option open to them to feel better about themselves. The lies we believe are so blatant, so obvious, it's amazing we don't notice them. However, with the liar hiding in other evil people alone, how could we see our complicity?

The truth is we are all responsible for the gang-rape-murder of Nirbhaya because we are all listening in the same way to a voice not our own that is hell bent on our destruction, whatever form it takes in our personal thoughts. Our insane and violent reactions to instances like this are no different to the instance itself. Reactions based on lies will never solve a problem based on lies. We cannot be condemned for our actions however, because we have no idea about this voice that commands us. None of us know what we are doing, or why.

Forgiveness is looking peacefully at, and understanding why, a person could not have known what she was doing when she did it. In all cases, it is because the liar is ruling the mind. Once we become clear about this there is hope, because once we know what the problem is exactly, we will have a chance to solve it.

Women do not rape; they do not have to rape or assert themselves sexually to prove their superiority. We all assume women inferior at some level and so there is not much to defend in any case. It is likely that the belief in inferiority and worthlessness support an inability to escape abusive relationships and impoverished lives. Whatever the situation, true strength - by definition - needs no defence. However, the women, men, and children that are raped and assaulted by men take the blame and society, dominated by masculine thinking, is unable to adequately address this incredible lunacy; and so it continues.

The first idea we ever have is *mother*. The abused and raped may be someone's mother. Ultimately, we are all each other's mother; that is the extent of our responsibility towards one another. We are all equal, all One, all Shakti. No one is different from any other and any label that assumes otherwise must be discarded.

There is no leap of faith required for forgiving a brother when we understand how the liar functions. It all makes perfect sense. It is natural to feel a deep sadness about the fact that us humans are so lost and unhealed right now but, at the same time, there is a profound compassion for those who have no idea what they are doing and so wantonly, ignorantly, go about destroying anything and everything in the way of their false-winner status.

Understanding the liar gives me hope. I am clear now on why the world is as it is and will continue to be so until we perform a collective healing of the human mind. Thankfully, some of us are starting this work in earnest.

The resistance to truly forgiving and undoing gender abuse, in all its forms, comes from our continued commitment to identifying with violent and aggressive labels on the one-hand, or victimhood on the other. Yet, none of these labels are true, and none of them we decided upon ourselves. This is the liar's game, now so easily seen. While we live in a world in which the majority supports an erroneous perceptual split, we must go quietly about our business knowing the truth without reacting angrily, or becoming frustrated with the time it is taking the others to catch up. They will catch up, without doubt. In the meantime we never have to accept the error ourselves again.

NIRAMISA WEISS

7 ABORTION

No woman actually wants to have an abortion.

The way some people speak, you might think that hoards of *evil* women are out and about and having sex irresponsibly in an attempt to get pregnant so they can have an abortion. This idea is clearly insane. There is, of course, the chance that a seriously unstable mind might be mad enough to put life at risk in this way, but it would be a most unusual case which we could immediately put down to extreme fear pressures invoking a total lack of mental stability, thus inducing extremely psychotic thinking and behaviour. Nevertheless, the premise that women are wantonly having unprotected sex, willy-nilly, just because an abortion is available is nonsense. Somehow, the arguments against abortion seem to suggest these ideas are true, but on a closer look they are simply covering the liar's tracks again.

To imagine that a person would actively seek the experience of abortion for herself and her unborn child is a particularly deranged idea. The idea arises from the anger generated by the belief that unborn humans should be safe from murder. This belief is fair and justified, but instead of calmly looking at the problem in order to understand it and so find a solution, we seek to blame alone. Our angry reactions billow out, turn violent, aggressive, and irrational, and eventually develop into wilder forms of the liar's tantrums; tantrums which have led to the justification for murder in defence of the *pro-life* label. All this is the liar's business, taking another, particularly sad form. It is total insanity, of course, but also an extreme example - and therefore useful in that we might more easily see - of how the liar in our minds forces us to behave as badly as those we believe worse than us.

It is true that the murder of the unborn is a tragic act that no-one sane would wish to carry out. It is also true that it is happening, constantly, without cessation, across the world, whether it is illegal or not; and it has been ever since we were able to figure out how to do it. It's a very sad state of affairs but none of us want to look at it carefully, let alone take any responsibility for it, so we point the finger and label desperate people as *evil*, or support its continuance, as if it were OK.

Neither of these standpoints is a solution to the problem, so the liar maintains the conflict *and* the murder; a win-win indeed.

We must see that we are all complicit in this particular lie, as we all support the continuance of a world in which abortion is the only escape from impossible situations arising from actions caused by our own, deeply-cherished, erroneous beliefs. In particular, we are talking about the belief in gender inequality and the unquestionable right of men to own and control objectified women, and thus do whatever they want with them without worrying about the effects. Furthermore, we *all* share these beliefs.

The group that *currently* claims the liar's label of *victim, worse-than,* and *owned/objectified* experiences the untenable situations that must inevitably arise from this labelling. Women can gain a little personal power, and an apparent escape from suffering and fear, in the form of more suffering and fear, via murdering their own children through abortions and other family planning activity.

The liar's work is in building perceptual guilt machines, and abortion is one of its biggest successes. Having already been slathered with the required amount of guilt, in many cases, the solution to an unwanted pregnancy is worse than the problem itself; women are regularly maimed and killed through abortion procedures. Notice, too, that we never consider the actions of the male as significant in all this madness. Abortion is the sad best effort we have come up with for fixing the inevitable mess made by our insistence in perpetuating owner/owned, simian-like, unconscious sexual relationships within a newly aware human consciousness.

In a world in which *he* who fucks the most is the winner, and that *she* must be owned by a *he* and be fucked by *him* whenever *he* likes, *she* will tend to have zero input in her own fate. An object owned has no real autonomy or personal decision-making capabilities. For female animals, continuous pregnancy is the norm. For female humans, then, unwanted pregnancies are inevitable. This is not conjecture; it is the way of our world; whether we are talking about pregnancy arising through rape and prostitution, or from a woman's psycho-emotional inability to insist on contraception if a man would rather do without.

If we resist looking at the facts, we are merely protecting them and the only reason we might do so is due to a false sense of being better than all this. This better-than state needs a lot of defence because it is simply not true. Let's drop the falsehood now and accept that we all still behave like monkeys, at whatever intensity and at least perceptually.

From having sex with strangers in broad daylight on the Brazilian streets at carnival time, to lying back and thinking of England for a few seconds, to indulging in sadomasochistic novels and stories, our sex lives present no evolutionary advancement at all. When we accept this is the case, we can start to change our minds entirely about what we are. Furthermore, it is only by changing our minds in this way that the world might become a peaceful and joyful place, where all new arrivals are welcomed, loved, and cared for.

Abortion is everyone's fault because we have not looked at the thinking behind it, let alone attempted to heal it in any way. We assume that we are sane and that everything is OK, against the preponderance of evidence to the contrary. Abortion is just another sneaky way the liar has managed to project the blame for our messed-up thinking regarding sex and partnerships onto women alone. In fact, all family planning activities assume the way the world is set up perceptually is reasonable and never to be questioned. Yet when there is no autonomy for the female, even in the subtlest sense, then it will be nearly impossible for her to assert herself in terms of the control of sexual activity, or protect herself against disease and unwanted pregnancy. Interestingly, the pill deals with the pregnancy issue marvellously, as does any form of contraception that is administrated away from the masculine view. If women's reproductive issues can be dealt with external to the sexual act itself, then the whole business can maintain its animal-like weirdness.

It reminds me of someone I met recently who had been working with NGOs in Thailand, set up to help poor women avoid the lure of the sex *industry* - a bizarre way of renaming something repugnant in order to make it sound reasonable and justified, must be the liar again. These organisations are putting a lot of effort into making farming appear an attractive lifestyle so that poor Thai women won't be seduced into the cities by the call of the Western white-male's wallet, and some may even be tempted back home from there. That was the idea. Well, it seemed ridiculous to me that all this frenetic charitable activity was attempting to fix what, in truth, isn't broken. As if raising the day rate for a farm worker from $5 to $10 might persuade women not to bother going into the city to have sex with strangers and earn $100 in a day instead! We have totally missed the point on this, and on all issues based on sex and gender, in all cases and everywhere in the world, as we might expect given our minds are not our own.

When it comes to the deep perceptual splits of which we are only half aware - mistakes in thinking that cause real suffering in the world - the liar persuades us to not look at the problem itself and instead focus on something barely related to it. Like a car which gets a puncture, we are assured that by changing the headlight we will be addressing the real problem. We are also assured that we will be recognised by the others as being *very good people* (better-than) for having done so.

Currently, all humans are insane, regardless of gender. Women rarely know what they want or don't want, but they are more likely to defer to the male, he who is perceptually in charge. This idea is legislation in some countries, like Afghanistan for example, but is also acceptable in the most *enlightened* civilisations. Whoever we are and wherever we live, we share belief systems based on gender inequality that we inherited from the apes. Any attempt to redress the inequality most often reaffirms the values of the masculine precepts of dominance and control. Thus, *unforgivables* like abortion remain the only option for a great many helpless people and the screaming and suffering world as we know it remains unhealed.

Abortion is the liar's invention and it must be delighted with it indeed. Not only does it ensure the *evilness* of women and their indisputable sexual deviance, it manages to kill bodies, endlessly. What success it has had with its dark scheming, right under our noses; none of us realising we live under a mental dictatorship that seeks to split apart, destroy, and kill. Not even the winner is safe. The liar has certainly not reserved the pleasure of mass murder for men alone.

The female human has no autonomy under the liar's dictatorship and, if she dares to take some for herself, woe betide her. In more feral societies today, women may be stoned to death for the most trivial things, such as having mobile phones. These cultures offer us extreme proofs of the beliefs we all hold to be true at some level. While women are being killed for nothing in Pakistan, and assuredly many Pakistani women are agreeing to such things, even if just tacitly and silently, Western women are obsessed with how sexually appealing they are and have become addicted, in their millions, to books which tell stories about women, just like them, being punished by men. There is no real difference in the content; the belief in the necessity of punishment for the worse-thans. The form varies, as with all of the liar's projections, but the content, and so meaning, stays the same. The liar punishes all worse-thans, as a defence against any questioning of the false label.

We are made up of worse-than and better-than, and the worse-than should definitely suffer for being so. We rarely get to see that the liar's assurance of a better-than state is, in truth, unachievable. There is *only* a worse-than state in the liar's world, with better-than beliefs trying, hopelessly, to cover it up. The liar promises a better-than state and then bids us spend every breath in attempting to achieve it. These attempts include the destruction of those which we believe are worse than us. We are assured that by destroying them we will overcome our fear and be safe. But it is a liar, after all, and we have never once felt safe yet. The liar's one true goal is suffering and death for all, no exceptions.

Although it is the masculine that is saddled with the need for aggression, fear, and violence, the feminine has done very little to advance the species either, choosing to go along with and put up with things as they are, and in some cases defend the status quo as fiercely as any bloodthirsty warrior might defend his land. Perhaps this is simply a side-effect of the lack of autonomy of an object. An object owned cannot decide its own fate or make its own decisions. An object owned survives at the whim of its owner. Accepting things as they are is all a non-autonomous conscious being might do - like children without any input in government. And let's face it; it's been an eye blink since women got the vote.

Whatever the *unforgivable* event we are looking at is, the liar insists we avoid addressing the insanity itself. Instead, it persuades us to attack mercilessly those desperate ones who are led into regrettable activity by being unable to assert themselves against the deeply held - and carefully learned - belief in their own powerlessness. In the same way that the women of Pakistan may agree to the stoning of their mobile-phone-owning sister, we save all the guilt for those labelled worse-than, and no punishment is too harsh. Western charities report on such horrors in brutal societies while avoiding highlighting the gender significance too much. Maybe these organisations discovered that mentioning the obvious gender issue lowered the donation rate. Again, we are all complicit because we all prefer to deny the obvious.

Abortion is a great way to continue labelling women as worse-than, *evil*, and keep them that way. As long as abortion is the only best hope for so many millions around the world, our unequal world will continue to spin out of control. Yet, finally, we are waking up. It is clear to our newly opening eyes that we have an awful lot of work to do. We must start by accepting all human beings as inherently equal, as if there were a law giving every human being in the world a divine state of equality. The equality of humans should be an unquestionable truth that can be counted upon, regardless of the specific circumstances of people's lives.

This is the beginning of perceptual change, which is where any change begins.

When we see that the belief in inequality, alone, has built our world with its countless problems and is a lie in every sense, perhaps we might then be able to discard it. When we discard the belief in gender inequality, we will also let go of the need to own, or be owned by, another body. We will let go of the desire to assert ourselves over the *powerless* or to be punished by the *powerful*. The belief in sex as some sort of necessary relief reserved for men alone - which if true would have perhaps brought a sense of responsibility along with it - can be discarded too. In fact, all the nonsense around sex that we accept without question will drift away into nothingness.

A world that accepts all people as inherently equal is currently unimaginable, as we have built everything we know on the liar's foundations of separateness. However, if we wrote international legislation that supported a divine right to equal humanness, that would be a start, even if just symbolic. When we can accept the equality of all our fellows, whoever and wherever they are, horrors like abortion will become a forgotten nightmare.

Life without the liar supports a world in which all babies are welcome and, on arrival, are cared for, cuddled, and loved unconditionally. Our world without the liar is one in which not a single baby is created through an act of self-loathing, violence, or hatred, subtle or not.

8 HOMOSEXUALITY

Closely related to the lie of gender and the conflict raging on incessantly due to our body differences, is the lie of sexual preference. I say *lie* because the liar uses this preference successfully to split us apart and set us against each other, as per its one function.

Along with all manner of physical things that appear to distinguish us as different from the others, the type of human we prefer to copulate with splits us into even more groups and subgroups, each group subject to evaluation by the others, and each group most certainly containing humans we believe to be fundamentally unequal to the rest. However, as with all the other lies we believe, pure human consciousness remains untouched by labels which may swap their meaning in an instant. Furthermore, what a person chooses to do, or not do, can never make them unequal. Moreover, the idea that a peaceful personal preference can render us worse than the others is a nonsense that we must discard.

We have already reasoned successfully against the liar in our minds in a number of arenas just like this one, without being aware of it. For example, the preference another person might have to food does not cause too much consternation these days, while in certain countries it is still difficult to ask for a vegetarian option without eyes rolling. We care little about how we prefer to dress in the West, not forgetting it was not so long ago when there were uproars over the wearing of short skirts. Let's not forget our fellows in foreign countries either, forced under threat of severe violence and murder to cover themselves from head to toe due to body differences; although I hear that underneath such coverings, extreme fashion preferences still reign supreme.

Things are changing in the world, without doubt. We have made great leaps towards a perceptual equality in recent times, particularly in the West; other parts of the world slowly catching up. Those peoples that lag behind, remaining in the grip of more extreme levels of fearfulness, serve as a reminder as to where we all were not so long ago. Something is also happening, generally and globally, around gender. We can't help but notice the changes in our perceptions of gender and its meaning. However, like any big change, it is all rather inexplicable from within, while it's happening. In any case, even though we most certainly are living in interesting and swiftly moving times, cultural changes are not what this book is about.

Homosexuality (and lesbianism, but to a lesser degree) is in this book about forgiveness because the idea has provoked so much anger over the years, inciting the justification of violence and murder. Personally, I struggle to understand the insane thought processes that condemn gay people in this way, but this is due to where and when I was born, my personal upbringing and life experiences. Still, I'm sure we are all aware of at least one person who still draws a sharp intake of breath at its mention and common insults across the board regularly use denigrating words reserved for homosexuals.

Sexual preference is used by the liar as a separating quality; a label, just like any other. There is no difference between believing that it is justified to kill people from another country, to rationalising attack on men who prefer sex with other men. Condemnation and justification of violence comes from hatred built up by divisive labelling, them and us; that which the liar uses most effectively, whenever and however it can, and especially whenever it has a fearful, willing ear. Them and us is an abstract prejudice that takes form in a peculiarly arbitrary manner. It can be as absurdly expressed as hating someone for using hand gestures in a particular way, or touching their nose when they speak, or something as irrelevant as that; and we all have our little pet hates like those, don't we?

We all share the liar and it is a success in all our minds, with no exceptions. When it manages to persuade someone to kill another person for a bizarre and meaningless reason, it must be very pleased with itself indeed.

The idea that there is something *evil* about homosexuality, something that can justify homicide, is absurd. In the end, we all share equal human consciousness, no matter how we have taken form while we are here on Earth. Moreover, if a person is not hurting others by their preferences to sex, food, or clothes, who are we to poke our noses into their business or have an opinion about it. However, as I mentioned previously, we have to mention this one because it makes people so crazy.

Our children, very obviously, reflect and imitate our personal and cultural belief-systems. If you were to go into schools and eavesdrop, you would find yourself listening to barrages of insults, more often coming from the boys who are studiously learning and applying the culturally required, aggressive, masculine behaviour. Often, the insults and the relentless commentary refer to the others, the *them* - whoever that might be at the time - in sexual terms. *Gay* is one of the labels used the most frequently in schools by boys against other boys, school being an arena in which the liar needs not hide too much. Gayness, as a label for a bully's target practice, is a no-brainer and some children spend their whole school lives fending off such persistent abuse.

We can assume, with some confidence, that at least some of the parents of the scornful children will be spoon-feeding their offspring these hateful ideas at home; while their children, the loudest, most aggressive kids, will be followed sheepishly by the anxious, quieter ones who are terrified of being singled out for violence and abuse themselves. This is just another mini-mirror of our sorry world; a world in which the functioning of our education systems depends on threats and punishment, confirming to young minds, over and over, the indisputable reality of fear and its necessity. How mad we all are! This is the world we agree is normal; the world of violence, abuse, and domination; the world where the most aggressive and violent male is the unquestionable winner. This is the world we refuse to acknowledge, mirrored back at us by our depressed, anxious, and insane children who have been learning it more assiduously than their lessons.

The liar has such a powerful control over our minds we usually have no idea why we hate a particular label's representation so much. If we asked the most prejudiced why they hate homosexuals, would they have a rational answer? Of course not. The liar incites irrational hatred and conflict, and it does so by pointing to differences and assuring us that these differences make a person worse than us. We believe these notions without assessing them for the most basic reasonability. From persuading us of the worse-than state of another person, it is just a simple next step into justifying their destruction at our hands.

When the liar persuades us that a person is worse than us, it has proved to us our better-than state. We believe this unreservedly. We feel somewhat relieved, while neglecting to check whether or not we are better-than. That which is better-than, if it were truly superior, de facto, would not need to seek out the continued destruction of that which it believes is worse-than. It would not have to keep on proving itself, incessantly; the definition of who is worse-than at any one time shifting and changing like the moon. This better-than state we cling to requires constant vigilance and defence; such defence taking the form of abusing those whom the liar tells us are worse than us.

The liar's game is perfectly logical, yet utterly insane and meaningless. Whenever we take a rare moment to stop and look at ourselves and our perceived enemies with care, we must notice that we are all equally terrified and no side has won anything, ever. The truth is that all of us are losers in this game; the most conspicuous loser is that person who believes he is the winner by having successfully destroyed another person, or group of people. Whatever the justification is for singling out people for bullying, violence, and murder, the deep fearfulness of the attackers is glaringly obvious. We should take note that the liar's voice is most effective when talking to the immensely fearful among us. In the end, it is impossible to single out any side for the label of victim. We are all victims of the liar's mental dictatorship, even when we are not personally involved in carrying out its dastardly orders, or are not at their receiving end either.

Like our definition of strength, which relies on the acceptance of an inherent weakness, the better-than state relies on an accepted and inherent worse-than state. We will never overcome this worse-than state, no matter how much false better-than is perceptually achieved. The confusions of meaning that turn reality upside down, dealt to us by the liar as givens and unquestionable, are behind all the suffering in the human world. It's not too difficult either to extrapolate these ideas into justifications for war, albeit in another setting with different players. The liar's ideas are simply varying forms of its one goal of splitting apart, separating, and destroying.

The blurring of our true mind with the liar's voice, and the belief that humans belong in groups of better and worse, digs the foundations for the eventual justification of genocide. If we are bashing gays, or gassing Jews, the fundamental psychotic reasoning is the same: the worse-than must be destroyed to maintain the feeble better-than state. Furthermore, whoever we label worse-than is an arbitrary matter as far as the liar is concerned; in 100 years, it could be white, male, wealthy heterosexuals if we don't do something to eradicate it soon. The liar's world proves the total insanity and deep lack of self-worth of *all* human beings, without exception. Whoever takes first place in the worst-than stakes is dependent upon nothing at all.

What the holy books from our global religions might say about homosexuality is more problematic. It must be met with nothing less than execution in some cases! Well, it wasn't so long ago that thousands upon thousands of women were burned to death at the stake for practicing a bit of herbalism. If we look back, and not even that far back, we can see an awful lot of seriously unpleasant human behaviour. In some places in the world such madness continues - madness seemingly better placed in far earlier epochs of human history.

As well as abstract spiritual teachings that remain valid over time, holy books also contain practical guides to life for humans at a *particular time*; these practical instructions are surely not meant to be followed for all eternity. Holy literature is always subject to change dependent upon the current power base; see, for example, in the Ramayana, the Islamic influenced rewrite of Sita's demise to account for Ram's missing *honour*, which translates to reworking the story in order that Ram may maintain his ownership of the sullied female in question by her suicide. Her misdemeanour was spending the night at another man's house!

So many things we *used to do* are out of the question these days, without much discussion. It is perhaps time to admit that what may have served to keep a feral populace in check many centuries ago is now out-dated, causing more problems than it resolves, even when reworked into complicated intellectual symbolism.

There is no area of human experience in which the liar is without control. Whenever we are persuaded to think we have found the answers to life, or peace and enlightenment, we are usually quickly shocked out of our reveries by alarming proof to the contrary. Sometimes we choose not to see what is in front of us, preferring instead to remain chained up inside worlds that insist that they hold the one, true key to freedom; becoming most defensive (attacking) when any alternative is suggested. Supporting the continuance of suffering in any form, in order to protect old and out-dated ideas out of blind respect for tradition or guru, simply seduces us into fiercely defiant *them and us* positions, all over again. From here, again, the justification of murder becomes easy. The liar's game is never ending.

The liar loves ideas that suit its own purposes, and was obviously involved in the writing or editing of the holy books. We can assume with some confidence that anything written in the holy books that instructs violence, murder, or even a minor unkindness is the liar's work. There's a lot of instruction to murder in the Bible. This is more than a little disappointing. Nevertheless, perhaps these were useful ideas at the time, serving to keep in check wilder, excessively fearful folk that may have exhibited behaviour even more inclined towards that of vicious, warring simians. Perhaps it was necessary to apply harsh laws until we found ourselves more easily able to reason and so pull back from violent and unconsidered reactions.

Surely, by now, it is clear to us that any human suffering is unacceptable, in whatever form it takes. We desperately need a collective peace of mind in order to eliminate suffering and feed everyone, for example, or even survive longer-term. If we take everything the holy books say as true we might have to bring a cow into the kitchen on a Monday morning as the dew falls at the gibbous moon, or whatever irrelevant nonsense. Nowadays, these things are impractical and nonsensical, so let's move on. The liar isn't too concerned with these non-conflict-inciting laws anyway, just the ones in which it can keep war and murder justified, in case you hadn't noticed. However, there is never any justification for hating our fellow beings. Hatred simply locks tightly shut our own perceptual cell door and, more often than not, such self-imprisonment has little effect on anyone else. Nevertheless, the incarcerated human mind, however damaging the external activities it suggests, is suffering and needs help and healing.

In a religious sense, then, the worse-than are those that fail to follow the prescribed mode of behaviour set out in the holy books, and so they are cast out by the majority unwilling to question the scriptures. The conflict easily spills over into the secular world and, wherever the worse-than find themselves, they harbour a deep sense of unworthiness due to their labels or preferences. Homosexual members of world religions suffer extraordinary levels of stress due to being unable to be open or honest about their feelings. Even so, the pain of denial is always far worse than any suffering that might arise due to a declaration of the truth. Indeed, the sense of freedom and relief that honesty brings turns people's lives around completely, and so many choose to be open about their feelings and bravely go against the collective liar-mind. Yet a strong sense of worse-than must remain, as these beliefs are powerful sorcery coming from the oldest of our traditions.

Roles are set in stone in the unexamined mind and when we step outside the perceived correct *way of things*, we risk attack. The lie that sexual preference can label us evil is just another morphing of the gender inequality lie, in which roles are set in stone and unquestionable. If a man dares to go against his own label, he must suffer the less-than (a man) fate, with all the punishment that comes along with it. However, again, if the superior are truly better-than, they would just let the rest get on with life. But they don't, they can't, because better-than is always a lie and so fear, anger, and attack arises to defend the lie from the truth of a more profound sense of personal or group unworthiness that is always bubbling just under the surface, ready to pounce at the slightest provocation.

Religions that outwardly promote fearfulness and punishment appear blind to what is going on in the world. Fear blinds and is oftentimes a deeply-engrained part of the set-up of a religion. From a peaceful perspective we may watch, detachedly, the screaming religious lunatics who cannot know what they are doing if they find themselves guided to represent love by its opposite.

There is something rather beautiful about this undeniable gender role-shifting experience we humans are having that deserves another word. We seem to be being drawn irrevocably to the uncomplicated, inherently equal, and story-less state of the consciousness shared by all, whether we like it or not. We are the lucky witnesses to the process of the evolution of consciousness.

We can assume that the vast majority of people, everywhere, would have considered homosexuality, lesbianism, and other variations of similar ideas *evil* in the not too distance past due to cultural norms. Nowadays, particularly in the West, we allow people to live their own lives peacefully. We rarely concern ourselves with each other's behaviour and preferences. This is clear proof as to how forgiveness is easy; a breeze indeed. We don't even know we are doing it, in fact, but it is what we have done with homosexuality, without the leap-of-faith the *religious* sort of forgiveness might require.

The truth is, we cannot help but forgive when we naturally consider all others as equal to ourselves, and due the same right to happiness. There is no effort required for forgiveness and the changing attitudes towards our homosexual brothers, over a very short time frame, are solid proof that humans *are* able to let go of old hatreds without strain and so forgive easily and with little trouble. We see too that our new arrivals do not pick up on old prejudices once they are cleared from group consciousness. Once forgiven, whole conflicts disintegrate and disappear; just like books like this, which will become unnecessary and irrelevant when we see all these unforgivables for what they are.

9 THE PAEDOPHILIA WITHIN THE CATHOLIC CHURCH

Before we become aware of the liar in our minds, something not yet forgiven has the power to gnaw away at us, causing us untold misery and pain. Before we are aware of the liar in our minds, true forgiveness - where our minds are completely free of upset like this - must come from a leap of faith. Many of us are finding that the faith we have in our fellow humans, which includes the belief in their inherent equality, is all that is required for discarding grudges and forgiving. Yet when it comes to bigger, more horrible situations, we often get into perceptual difficulties and usually end up relying upon the liar's form of forgiveness again which, as we have seen, is not true forgiveness at all as it insists upon punishment and the reality of eternal condemnation and *evilness*.

This is where understanding the liar, in its entirety, is indispensible. Knowledge of the liar and how it functions eliminates any need for faith in our brother as his equality has become an indisputable fact. We are left with no option but to see issues with which we previously had extreme difficulty as an inevitable and unavoidable part of our species-wide insanity. The leap of faith that has been required for forgiveness, up until now, is due to the fact our minds have been locked up inside the liar's shackles. When these shackles are seen for what they are, undone and discarded, no more faith is required. It is like accepting that the world is indisputably round.

Once we see the liar in action and can no longer deny its existence, the process of forgiveness becomes rather like describing a material object by its component parts; protons, neutrons, and electrons. It is as it is, and there is no question about it. We simply look at any issue we might be struggling with and apply the perceptual model of the liar to it. We are then able to describe, in a loving and compassionate manner, what happened and how our brother could have been mad enough to do it. Nothing at all can evade this sort of forgiveness, even that required by the paedophilia of a large number of priests within the Catholic Church.

You may have noticed there's been somewhat of a theme rolling along the last few chapters. It seems that the idea that sex is bad, without any real explanation as to why that is so, is very prevalent. A good place to start in our discussion of the intensely insane behaviour of apparently celibate priests could be an attempt to understand what this bizarre perceptual twitch is all about. In my first book, which describes the liar-mind in a more general sense, there are four successive chapters; *The Body, Gender, Relationships* and *Sex*. It is these themes in which the liar's business takes form in a very obvious manner.

Firstly, we believe we are bodies alone and that consciousness has arisen, by chance, from our physical constitution. In truth, it is the other way around, consciousness continuously finding better ways to express its union and oneness as we evolve. However, by misunderstanding what consciousness is, the body has become extremely important. From here, it is not too difficult to convince ourselves that we are completely alone, imprisoned in our skins, unable to truly know, or be known by, another. We die alone, we often say, the body's end considered ours too. This state of mind is so horribly fearful that we continuously seek to alleviate it, most often by searching for another person to join with.

This *separateness* we believe defines us brings with it a deep sense of lacking and sadness; that which no-one has been able to replenish. We feel that something very important is missing and we spend our days desperately trying to find this thing and so solve the conundrum of our lives. One of the most common ways in which we attempt to alleviate our isolation and become whole again is via partnerships with another person. These partnerships, we believe, are the answer to our problem. They may take form as a brief sexual fling, or a lifetime's marriage, but however they take form they never suffice to solve the riddle of humanity and we are still left feeling depressed and alone, even in the closest and most loving of family situations. Something extremely important is always missing.

Sex is a key focus of these unions that promise us happiness and peace. We believe we are bodies after all and it is most certainly the closest any two bodies can get to each other. We believe that by uniting sexually with another human being we will finally be happy and fulfilled. For a short moment, perhaps, we do find happiness and fulfilment. Sadly, it doesn't last, because if it did - if sex could solve the problem of our persistent loneliness - we wouldn't be so desperate to do it again with someone else at that inevitable moment when we begin to feel just like we felt before; lost and alone all over again, endlessly chasing bodies, false unions without end.

Sex promises the answer to everything; a resolution to all our sadness, pain, loneliness, and lacking. Yet the promise is a lie and, even though the deception is glaringly obvious, we ignore the truth and continue looking for peace in a place we will never find it. Whenever we avoid accepting the obvious, in any situation, our psychosis is compounded and our confusion multiplied. Feelings of isolation, abandonment, and betrayal cover the truth of our insanity and we quickly justify anger and hatred towards those we had previously reserved for saviour status. Reassigning that function we thought would save us as the chief weapon in our arsenal against those that would hurt us is an easy perceptual shift to make while our perception is in the grip of the liar.

Sex is one of many false alternatives to true happiness the liar offers. The liar knows what it is doing and, deep down, we know it too. Thus, in case we finally start to look in the right place for answers, the liar must be very vigilant and ensure we keep chasing bodies around. It has even persuaded some of us that through sex itself we might become spiritually enlightened. As if an orgasm could have external effects; magical orgasms that fantastically give us power over others. What a lunatic it is! And how mad are we to believe it.

These lies are obvious if we consider peace and joy as part of something non-physical; i.e. not from anything that the animals do. Like fasting, celibacy is supposed to transcend the physical desires and is part of all religious practices. However, whatever the reasoning behind instructing priests to remain celibate might be, as a religion grows and many are called to become its representatives, it is clear that many of these people are simply not equipped, qualified, or even remotely prepared for the life they have chosen to go into. We may well question the motives of those becoming priests as being entirely liar-backed too. Freedom from poverty, achieving a higher status in the community, a need to avoid addressing a preponderance of hateful (by the liar's standards) homosexual desires, a profound physical inadequacy, or any other non-spiritual factors, are inappropriate reasons for taking up a spiritual life, and trouble can be expected.

When something is forbidden, it gets the essence of being a *bad* thing. It could be anything at all; wearing red socks, for example. The intensity given to the label of *badness* denotes how much fear we will experience when we find ourselves in a situation that does not allow us to wear red socks. If someone was bound to whip us if we wore red socks, we might become terribly afraid at the thought of them. If someone ordered us to take them off if we dared to wear them, the threat of cold feet might get the better of our rebellious nature. However, on a warmer day, we might be inclined to find out what all the fuss is about. We may even develop an obsession or fetish for red socks. The seductive power of things forbidden can get awfully powerful in weak minds.

Christ may have been celibate, and he may not have been, we cannot say for sure. His disciples and followers most surely were not, on the whole. Even if the idea behind celibacy is reasonable, its requirement for priests of the Catholic Church has clearly been met with a vast amount of twisted dissension. We should state clearly that the Catholic Church is not the only religious organisation rotting inside in this way, but it has given us such a spectacular example of the inevitable misuse of power and bullying of innocents that must arise in such better-than groups, we use it here as an extreme example of this sort of *unforgivable*. We may also assume that it is not a new thing either. What is new, and wonderful, is the allegedly *powerless*, the *worse-thans*, the *victims*, are now finally able to speak up.

The lie that sex is *bad* and the flesh sinful, and all that nonsense, has caused such psychosis in apparent spokespeople for God, we are all amazed and saddened at their behaviour. We might reasonably ask if this behaviour has been the norm for many centuries, blind-eyes turned, power kowtowed to? In India, for example, apparently celibate holy men get away with sex crimes and even murder at times, and no-one wants to look at it, know about it, or do anything practical about it - as if it were the way of the world and to be expected and so condoned. Perhaps we used to think this way also. It was not so long ago that our parents would have beaten us had we told them the shopkeeper down the road had just sexually molested us.

Even so, something very interesting has been happening lately; a perceptual shift in the human world that has its beginnings in the West around the emancipation of women. Suddenly, out of the blue, it is no longer acceptable to put up with extreme levels of fear and bullying as this new voice of the previously voiceless drags the dark shadows of fearful deeds screaming into the light, the trailblazers permitting all *victims* everywhere to do the same, and so heal themselves and the world.

We are more aware of ourselves than ever before. Instead of being whisked away instantaneously by the liar's seductions we can pause, mid-thought, and ask if this particular course of action is sensible or not.

Unlike the plains' antelope in heat, we have the power to stop ourselves copulating endlessly. Yet, the liar's dark clouds continue to billow around sex. The desire for sex is felt viscerally. Lust is a strong, sometimes overwhelming, physical experience felt in the body. If we examine closely the feelings of any strong desire we might have, such as any addiction, including lust, we may notice the emotional feelings connected with the ideas are very apparent in the physical body; our hearts may pound, the hairs on our skin may become static, our mouths may become dry, and we may even feel physical pain. Interestingly, these are exactly the same physiological signals we recognise as fear.

From a broad perspective, we can see that the only thing holding us back from the next evolutionary step is fearfulness; the prerequisite for, and consequence of, believing the liar's ideas. It doesn't matter what form it might take or how justified it might be, fear is the only obstacle in the way of peace, be it personal peace of mind or world peace. The liar is a fear-based mental device, utilising human language for inventing, manipulating, and managing the fear already present and rehashing it into unlimited new forms, incessantly. When we look at life on our planet, we notice that fear is a common factor in the lives of all sentient beings, without exception. All life on Earth shares fear at varying levels of intensity, so all life on Earth shares the liar-mind too. It was able to manipulate language only at the human stage of evolution.

We humans have spent much time eliminating fear from our lives. Biologists say that our success in making safe havens for ourselves explains why our bodies are so weak and feeble when compared to our nearest evolutionary neighbours. This suggests we have been at this human life for far longer that we can imagine, or than our historical records purport. Due to our innovatory skills, we simply stopped needing to jump so high or bite so savagely in order to survive, and so our bodies grew into a form requiring less defence (fearfulness). We can see the remaining fear in open human conflict, and in the liar-mind chatter when we are watching closely enough.

However, a good proportion of human fearfulness has buried itself deep, hiding behind acceptable ideas, unquestioned emotions, and commonly experienced bodily feelings, while the liar's voice persuades us that these are desirable or necessities rather than fearful. This liar activity underpins the archetypal link between fear and desire that we must acknowledge from time to time. It follows, then, that any of the body feelings we mistake for a natural desire or a reasonable need must be fearfulness misconstrued. We can go even further and say that any feeling that takes root in the body somewhere *must* be a representation of fear; simply because we are not bodies.

Do you remember how falling in love feels? Maybe you are in love right now. Check your body for signs of this emotion taking root in physical feelings. For me, it was always a tingling in the stomach that told me something exciting was happening in my life, something good. I hadn't yet noticed that this feeling was exactly the same thing I felt when the emotional story around it was completely the opposite, something frightening, unwanted, and unpleasant. From the impending death of the body, the committing of a crime, the promise of romance, monetary gain of any sort, an addict's relief approaching, public speaking, or a difficult meeting coming up, for example, we experience the same physical feelings. Whatever we label the feeling to be, however, is simply a judgment; a story the liar tells us. The labelling of these feelings is arbitrary. However, these feelings do have one thing in common. They represent fear, even when we believe them to be beneficial.

These physical feelings lead us ever deeper into separateness, isolation, and conflict, and further away from peace; however we have labelled them and whatever we commonly considered them to signify. We are seduced by body sensations that seem to promise different things at different times, but ultimately always deliver the same result, destruction and disconnection. Feelings of lust, desire, and the overwhelming need to have sex, then, are representations of fear. They go hand-in-hand with the deep worthlessness we all feel at some level. Therefore, they subsequently offer us a manner of victimising and bullying others too. Sex is bad because what we believe about it is full of fear and conflict.

We know all of this, without knowing that we know. We are aware that we are hurting ourselves, over and over again. Nevertheless, instead of calmly seeing it all as a bad idea and changing our minds softly, quietly, and reasonably, the liar in our mind compounds our distress into shadowy symbols of power over others by their consumption in a sexual sense, and so promises the alleviation of our assured worthlessness. The liar persuades us into believing that we will be better than the others, and so find peace, if we pursue our body sensations to their bitter end. When we are the firm ally of the liar, better-than is our only goal and we will be unable to see sanity.

Therefore, sex is *bad*, and here we have our brother with no true spiritual calling; someone who spent most of his life feeling very insecure about himself, suddenly respected, admired, and looked up to by a whole community. While there, in safety and enjoying a delicious new feeling of dominance, he finds himself in a group of similarly-minded people who have convinced themselves that they are very much better than everyone outside of their small superior circle that, allegedly, has direct access to God Himself. This better-than belief, the new brother will take on with the speed of the starving at their first proper meal in weeks. No-one realises they are listening to a liar's ideas; that which tells them that everything they think and do now that they are priests, and therefore better than everyone else, is given the OK from the Big G upstairs. The liar very quickly gets the upper hand in environments such as this and it is not so long before the fear levels reach screaming proportions and the unthinkable becomes justified.

There can never be a justification for paedophilia, but somehow human manage to justify it to themselves. We will see a similar ability in the Nazis, who were suffering from such severe levels of psychotic better-than beliefs that were so obviously not true - even to them, at some level of consciousness - they had to be defended continuously. Anything can be justified under the liar's tutelage and, if the worse-than self-perceptions run very deep, the intensity of the activities designed to assuage them has no limit. Moreover, as we have seen, the liar's worst enemy is the innocent and what could be more innocent than a little child. The liar persuades its willing host to destroy the innocent and use sex as a weapon of fear and condemnation. Using sex in this way is not unusual in our sorry world but, due to the age and the innocence of the victims whose parents had entrusted into the care of God's delegates, this case takes the form of something practically impossible to understand and so becomes *unforgivable* in our unexamined minds.

Then, to whatever sick personal and group justifications the priests were able to muster to support these vile deeds, we must add the general misconception by Christians that crucifixion is the punishment we all deserve - missing entirely the lesson of eternal innocence, a successful liar reinterpretation if ever there was one. Confusing the message of the perfect human mind has caused so much misery in the Christian world and cannot be too far away from the systematic *punishment* of innocent little children by those given the power to do so. When the Catholic Church deems suffering a requirement, and innocent children are not yet suffering, an insane and faithful mind might justify supplying the lack of suffering while at the same time believing he is doing the right thing. The burning of witches, the forced enslavement of women, violent religious mortification, the systematic sexual abuse of altar boys, as well as all sorts of insane things we get up to in the name of God, are supported by the idea that we are poor pathetic sinners, requiring suffering, punishment, and crucifixion if we are to be saved.

If we are unable to see that the minds of these paedophile Catholic priests were so unhinged, so seriously psychotic - new carriers of the disease arriving wide-eyed daily to join a group already so profoundly sickened by the unrestrained power games indulged in for many centuries, millennia even - then we have to condemn our brothers as doomed to eternity. And this simply makes us as sick as them.

The Catholic Church asks us to forgive the paedophile in its ranks but has not attempted to understand what happened in order to heal; nor will it have much success in doing so while it is an organisation ignorantly dependent on many of the liar's ideas of inequality. Uncovering the liar, at the root, quickly reveals it wherever it might be hiding in our lives. Usually, this is difficult to admit. We usually become angry and defensive against the idea that there is something wrong with us. This is just the liar protecting itself again. After serious consideration, undoing the liar starts to appear reasonable, useful, and helpful at the very least, and so we place our focus onto healing certain areas of our lives, while assiduously avoiding others. Wherever we find ourselves becoming angry, frustrated, irritated, and upset is where the liar is still in residence. It may take some time to be able to face up to the fact that all our self-destructive thinking is undesirable.

My teacher assures me that if we cherish even a tiny bit of the liar's thinking, we keep it all. This is because the liar's thinking is simply one horrible idea taking form in innumerable ways, each form just another representation of the original error. Thus, the process of attempting to resolve only a select few of the liar's sick machinations usually implodes. Our attempts at fixing isolated problems can achieve temporary solutions but eventually they will rear up again elsewhere in another form. Ultimately, a full unmasking of the liar will reveal its activities everywhere and any organisation built on better-than, worse-than ideals will have to heal, change, and evolve, or die as per its sponsor's world-view. We will not be able to resolve systemic paedophilia, or any type of abusive behaviour in any organisation, without first addressing the deeply embedded liar beliefs that allow its justification in the minds of those seduced into treading these dark paths. Furthermore, we will have to address all lies accepted as true by the group mind of the organisations protecting these activities.

On discussion about this forgiveness work, people sometimes ask: *What about the victims? What if they can't forgive? Isn't that important?* The assumption being that if the victims don't forgive then we can't either, as if we should reserve forgiveness for *victims* alone. This is rather illogical given that some will forgive and some won't; some will forgive next year and some in ten years and some not in this lifetime. Let's write off the need for the victim to take the lead in forgiveness. Time-based compassion is conditional love and therefore sits deeply within the liar's belief structures. However, we all need peace of mind now, whoever we are and whatever our connection to such incidents. Furthermore, we are all evolving at different speeds, so let's get on and forgive the moment we can and stop wasting precious time.

Until we have forgiven, and forgiven properly, whoever we are - innocent, paedophile, onlooker - we are under the liar's dictatorship; that which insists on the reality of sin, the impossibility of healing, and an eternity of condemnation. Condemnation is obviously no solution to anything, no matter how much we love to indulge it. Yet we must also be compassionate and understanding with those in pain and unable to find peace, offering our help when they ask for it. We all have a part to play in forgiving the unforgivable while the liar rules the human perception. Fixing our thinking will mean that all unforgivable actions stop and become part of a vague nightmare from centuries gone by; like so many other things we simply don't do any longer.

We must also ask ourselves honestly, who is the true victim? Is it the abused innocent child, his due enjoyment of life violently ripped away from him; is it the lunatic priest, powerless against the screaming voice of destruction; or is it all of us while any iota of the liar's madness remains reasonable. The truth is that we are all interlinked to everything that happens in the human world and, while any of us remain insane, humanity is not healed or free and paedophilia will continue to be justified in intensely fearful minds; minds psychotic enough to believe these horrible actions offer them personal relief from their own fearfulness.

Those of us living comfortably outside these *unforgivable* circles of tragedy believe we are sane and better-than in comparison; as if we had never used our advantage over a person with less resources to mitigate our own anxiety, even if the resource in question was simply confidence. We are mostly hypocrites who have not yet looked at our own thinking properly and it is high-time we did.

The notion of *victim* is powerful sorcery and, even though it is not clear if one person could be hurting any more than another, we reserve the bulk of the pain for the victim; assured of their sorry, worse-than state and unable to look them in the eye. This is our share of the guilt we project onto them because we believe exactly the same lies as the sexual deviant, albeit at a lesser intensity. We are implicated yet again. Our own unexamined, liar-mind thinking assures us that a victim of sexual abuse has shouldered the burden of guilt, even when they are tiny children. The ease in which sexual deviants, bullies, and abusers of all types can carry on their dirty work, while their victims are unable to speak up, has everything to do with the liar's labelling of the victim of sex crimes as guilty; the victims themselves accepting this sick definition.

We are able to take practical action to help people suffering in the world as long as we are sure they accepted no guilt. If we are unsure about this, we may hold back our kindness. We do not tarnish victims of a serial killer in the same way we do victims of a rapist, for example, those considered to carry the blame for the crime. We do not ask the robbery victim taking the stand why he was walking through that dodgy area of town late at night. We do ask the underage, tearful girl what colour knickers she was wearing that morning at home.

Boys abused by holy men may spend the rest of their lives in mental torment, not knowing if they might be homosexual or not, a notable proportion of them committing suicide to escape the pain of their unresolved experiences. The inability of the abused to do anything about an abusive situation is often compounded by the fact that the abuser is a well-respected member of the community, perhaps having a large congregation, or many thousands of devotees, who would most likely beat someone before considering their beloved could behave in such a manner. It is only the belief in the projection of guilt that causes these tragic examples of our insanity.

The victims are the innocent ones, remember? Even so, they don't believe it either. It is not what any of us heard repeatedly about how the world functions. It is often safer for an abused person to keep quiet about their experience than to tell someone who we would hope might be able to help them; the threat of abandonment by those closest to them far worse than anything they might have experienced already. Sometimes, the fear can be so acute, a person may deny the memory of abuse entirely. It is a lie that a person can suffer from the projected guilt slathered by a sexual psychopath, but the world believes otherwise, even parents, and even when the abuser is a regular criminal and not a holy person.

In spite of what we believe, it is impossible to share guilt because guilt doesn't exist; it is a lie. Guilt relies upon the reality of sin and eternal condemnation, but these cannot exist in truth. We are simply making terrible mistakes due to believing a voice of doom which took control of our thoughts a long, long time ago. Mistakes can be corrected and correctable mistakes imply no guilt at all. The idea that the innocent can be smeared with the guilt of another is ludicrous, in fact. It is nonsense, but we all believe it to be true and so unforgivable acts continue to be justified in the fearful human mind that believes the impossible has happened and that the innocent must be punished. We have built a world with this madness at its core that is, in truth, a total illusion.

The liar insists upon the reality of guilt, knowing that without it, its demise is assured. Guilt is the liar's fuel and, in order to keep filling up, it assures us endlessly that through the projection of guilt we may relieve ourselves of our personal terror. We act upon this lie from the moment we are able to. *He did it*! we yell, pointing to our younger sibling as the wooden spoon is brandished again, threatening more tears and red bottoms. *She did it!* bellows the barrister, pointing to the teenage girl who decided to wear red, frilly knickers that day. *Liar!* thunders the priest, tarnishing the bravest altar boy who dared speak up. We all share the psychosis that builds our world. Undoing our collective psychosis on guilt, and all liar-mind devices, will free victims of abuse from the eternity of doom they believe they are due. It will also free the abusers, because they too are innocent.

In self-help and spiritual circles, we are told that our lives and relationships falter because we look to the past and cannot forgive what we see there. We learn that now, the present moment, is the only reality we have and, therefore, we can discard past and future. After a short time, we realise the self-help books are correct as we notice we spend our thinking entirely on regretting our painful past or hanging onto wishful dreams for the future that never transpire. When we stop indulging the past, we can let it go and enjoy a more positive life experience. When we ditch the need to control the future, our lives become lighter and more joyful. This can all be extrapolated into the collective consciousness with some ease. In an evolutionary sense, the fear we brought with us from past states of consciousness - that which we can see in action in our nearest simian neighbours - is now extraneous and unnecessary.

We are unaware of the perceptual evolutionary step we have taken and are actually still moving through it; although preferring to arrogantly consider ourselves the end result, a job well-done. As a species we live through uncountable stories of fear and suffering, of separateness and loneliness, of better than and worse than; the nature of which has been completely overlooked, up until now. We are perpetual story-tellers but all our stories share the same deep lacking, the same mistaken self-identification. When the fear in our stories becomes truly intense, the form they take can become grotesque and horrifying. When the level of fear is manageably comfortable, we end our lives having wasted our time and experienced nothing of our true potential.

The fear of human beings is simply the same fear that all life on Earth shares, having added language and ideas to reshape more bestial conflicts into limitless forms. Fear is our problem. Fear is the older evolutionary state that we must now discard. However, the liar in the mind insists on fear. It insists fear is real, solid, and cannot be overcome. We believe this lie so heartily we do not even look at trying to heal fearfulness, as if it were impossible. Instead, we change the headlight bulb instead of the burst tyre and carry on down the road, eventually wondering why the vehicle is practically unusable and ready for the junk yard after such a short time.

The truth is, we are the missing link but, while fear remains, our confused state of being remains interminable and we will not know our true identity. As long as we are fearful, the unforgivable continues and we will never resolve the problems that we face. Once we let go of the need for fear, we will no longer project it into the world or require its representations in the body. This fear-free perceptual state of being is currently unimaginable. We are so limited, so small, so pathetically minded, we cannot envision how marvellous a world without fear could be. When we do get a glimpse of fearlessness - and we have all experienced this at some point in our lives - it seems miraculous to us simply because it is so strange.

The truth, when we experience it, seems like magic, it is so bizarre and unusual. It is calm, quiet, and welcoming, like nothing we have ever known before. It assures us that each of us is innocent and pure. It assures us that anything lamentable we have ever done was simply a mistake caused by believing a voice not our own; a voice that doesn't

84

exist. Truth assures us that we will all be free of fear eventually, inevitably.

10 SUICIDE

Humans are so unwittingly harmful it seems that, without knowing it, every decision we make, alone or as part of a group, has a fundamental element of destruction within it. I don't think we intend to destroy the planet with our activities, but it is inevitable as long as we think the way we do. I don't think we intend on divorce when we say *I do*, but it is inevitable as long as we think the way we do. We are just bodies anyway; fragile, prone to ill health, and bound to die sooner or later, and this makes life seem like a ridiculous joke sometimes. *Why bother with anything at all when we are just going to die and that's that?* we ask ourselves quietly and often, the lack of a reasonable answer serving as an excuse for even more senselessness destruction and profiteering.

Everyone knows someone who has an exceptionally low opinion of themselves, for whatever reason. It seems that everything that happens to this person is proof of their low opinion of themselves. There is always something *bad* going on, which they are often over-keen on relating, as if the juice of tragedy was a kind of tonic. If there isn't anything bad going on at present, there will be a relied-upon drama on the horizon, just to spice things up a bit. We may even witness them organising and planning the disaster, well in advance of the tears and upset. They appear completely oblivious to these logical and unemotional processes; even when, after they break up with their partner most acrimoniously, they crash the car the very next day.

They play continuous petty power games with their closest friends; the winning of which they hope will alleviate the dull pain of such low self-esteem. Our sociopathic friend smears those fleeing the toxicity with accusation and calumny which might offset any tricky questions. On the odd day in which everything is going well and they are feeling happy and bright - and as long as these happy moments are not false joy based upon the lies and destruction that is believed to be the foundation of life - good things do seem to happen. Yet, the world is still considered external to thought and so good things are seen as just more proof that success and happiness must come from outside; usually by *getting lucky* or getting someone to do something for them without having to make any effort in return.

We just described each other. We are all like this, at varying levels of intensity. Whatever we believe is reflected back to us by the world. When we start examining our thoughts, we can't help but notice this obvious process. That really bad day we're having is just an external projection of our inner turmoil. That difficult friend simply holds a mirror up to our own behaviour. This isn't even particularly wacky anymore and we all agree on the veracity of stress related illness. If something is bothering us, badly, it can have a very detrimental effect, even making us ill. The lie of separation is further debunked by the effect we have on the people around us, especially when we are extremely angry, for example.

We who are careening through our lives at the whim of the liar are not usually aware that our thoughts and beliefs tailor our life experience, but it is so. The liar offers us a seemingly bespoke design of personal suffering and we accept it greedily, always hungry for more. However, we share every desperate, wailing, sad, angry, suffering, or lonely thought with everyone else. There are no private or unique thoughts, in fact. The truth is we are not alone at all; we share everything, the good and the bad. The liar might want us to think that its ideas are inventive and interesting, but actually it is just chugging out the same tired old commands to war and conflict to everyone else too. When we see that the world's mirroring process is real, it is just a tiny step further to realising that we have the power to change things. Eventually, we will see that no destructive thoughts - those we thought were entirely unique to ourselves - are original or true and that they can all be discarded.

When we believe the world loves us unconditionally; that we are always cared for and tenderly looked after; that there is always enough to go around and that everything we do is blessed and for our own benefit and well-being; our experience of life reflects these wonderful truths back at us. From personal experimentation and experience, I can say that whatever I believe to be true proves itself to me, regardless of the evaluation. This must demonstrate our function of co-creator. But it is also, currently, further proof of the liar's overwhelming success in limiting our potential to its bare minimum. When we're happy, the world is a great place to be. Yet when the liar has the upper hand, persuading us that everything is wrong and it's all someone else's fault, the world can become a nightmare.

Whether we have a bad day or a good day may seem to be a random matter, but let's not forget Heaven.com and the perceptual software virus from Chapter Two. We should also take note of the energy and exertion required for maintaining a negative state of mind. More importantly, we should notice the calm and relief that comes when a positive and optimistic view arrives to take its place. And did we mention that those negative states can cause illness and the positive states avert it? It seems like the good stuff is easier and certainly needs far less defence. So how can the bad days retain any desirability at all? Well, little by little, as we start detaching ourselves from our self-identification with the liar and its destructive whims, they don't. Instead, what we start to notice, marvellously, is that whatever we preferred to see instead of the truth was the very thing that hurt us. We are the true authors of our own lives.

The beliefs we have that go against peacefulness make our lives hell, literally. One of the most problematic beliefs we have is that we are just a body, destined for annihilation. This belief, in the limitless forms it takes, causes us much distress. The success of neuro-linguistic programming and self-help affirmation practices comes from retraining the mind to believe the opposite of what it previously held true. Thus, if the mind is in a constant *poor-me* loop, we simply change the record and start to tell ourselves how amazing and wonderful we are; how grateful we are for the unlimited blessings we receive each day; how much we love ourselves; and more forms of this type of positive personal opinion. We do this regularly and, lo and behold, our life experiences change accordingly and start to prove our new mantra to us. We may even like to repeat to ourselves daily: *I am not a body. I am not a body.* This mantra has been very helpful for me.

To arrive at this stupendous and miraculous state of mind, which is still peppered with moments of slippage back into liar-mind perceptual patterns, one must traverse through the hell we have made for ourselves and see it for what it is. We certainly must walk through the valley of death before we can find our way out to the other side and freedom. However, when enough of us have made the crossing safely, the next generations will not be born into the same hell we were, and so they will not have to suffer it like we are doing now. This is surely a responsibility worth taking on. Currently, we all live in the valley of death, without knowing it. For too long we have lived in this dreadful place built on fear, not knowing where or what we are, refusing to become aware of the awfulness of our predicament, and not having the faintest inkling that we can change it all at any moment.

Propitiously, some of us have noticed the dire state of things and, by accepting the world as it is, we have stopped distracting ourselves with nonsense and start looking for a way out. Some of us have found peace of mind and a potential solution. Those people are obliged to tell the others what's going on. The reason for this is that freedom is completely useless alone. The idea of being free and happy, all alone, is the liar's idea. We may be happy and we may be peaceful but, as long as anyone else is still suffering, our work here is not done. The idea that enlightenment, or spiritual freedom, is a personal, singular business has more than just faint whiffs of the liar's model of better-than, worse-than, loser-winner; the winner, presumably, being the one and only enlightened one with no-one else able to achieve such an elevated state. Fortunately, all this is just more of its rubbish. Once we know what's going on, sharing our joy with those who might be ready to accept it too is a daily blessing. However, the journey is not easy and, because we must throw out so many things we deeply cherish in error, we may falter repeatedly.

With the liar in charge we cherish the world as it is. We believe in its goals and measures of worth and success and we give them a value they do not deserve. Everything the liar insists is important, we too believe to be important. If we are serious about getting out of this mess, however, all the things we have cherished for lifetimes, clinging onto as the demarcation of happiness and peace, we will have to discard. We must start seeing the ideas of the liar's world for what they are, lies. This can be excruciating.

My teacher tells me that a slow approach to truth is sometimes necessary because a sudden change of mental state into peace can be too much and we might become extremely distressed - inconsolable even - perhaps seeking to end our own lives. If someone took our beautiful little baby from us, we may well feel suicidal. When the truth threatens to rob us of our nightmare world of lies - that which we believe defines us - we may well feel suicidal.

As truth dawns, there can be short periods of deep depression, interspersed with ever-growing periods of peaceful joyfulness. The depression and angst signifies that something big is being discarded by the mind; some nasty belief that had underpinned our existence is being ripped away. Our thought-systems, and so lives, were built around the reality of this self-identification, so its departure is always temporarily painful. However, this pain is *always* temporary and we can welcome it as an indubitable assurance of peace to come.

Most of us who remain unaware of the liar, avoiding our personal healing work, are continually depressed, frustrated, and miserable, at varying levels of intensity, without knowing why or even recognising that we are unhappy. For some of us, the mental pain we are enduring is so extreme, the liar is able to be completely honest with us for a change, stating clearly its one and only true intention; and so it may seduce us into taking our own lives.

Nevertheless, it remains possible, at any moment, for anyone to make that short perceptual jump into truth. With every decision we make, the universe rearranges itself, offering the best possible path to freedom going forward. In each moment, instantaneous freedom is offered. We rarely take up the offer, but it is there. For most of us, the sudden jump into truth would be too painful, too overwhelming, and so we avoid it until such time as we are ready.

We might notice that those who have recently made the jump into freedom usually recount the process as having begun at the point of reaching the worst point of their lives, a place in which nothing in the world had any importance to them anymore; the darkest pits of personal suffering. Ironically, the liar's deepest dungeon cells are where we are able to let go of its reality more easily because, perceptually, there is nothing left to lose. For the rest of us, the process is slower; throwing out one false belief at a time, each one causing us difficulties as we begin to see it with new eyes, all pain disappearing once the conflict-free truth is accepted.

As we step more squarely onto the path of sorting out the true from the false in our minds, we become surer of ourselves, recognising that discarding a lie may hurt a little but certain that the pain will pass. At this point there is a strong inclination - liar suggested of course - to become enchained in the process of undoing, the liar having redefined it for its own ends. The liar insists that, due to the belief in our own worthlessness which we haven't yet entirely abandoned, the process of healing will be eternal and we will therefore never be free. It insists there is always something else to heal; that our personal pot of sin will never be empty. This belief is comforting to minds accustomed to lies and self-debasement. The liar is so smart it is able to reshape itself into new models of perception very easily. It will take what we thought was the way to freedom and manipulate it into the same old specialness and inequality. It is something we must become aware of and turn away from immediately when we see it.

With each scrapped lie, we are left with a quiet sense of wonder we have never known before. The dark clouds of suffering are gently wiped from our vision and we finally experience the beauty and stillness of a mind at peace with itself. We know our path is finally set, there is no going back. We know that we will be truly free. We can even see the whole way out of hell. There is no more doubt in our hearts. The next step is so clear. There is another state of consciousness, ready and available for all human beings; a conscious state of peace, love, knowledge, and togetherness. And we're so close and, then,... BAM! ...we're back into guilt, and back into the liar's fakery as we come up against another false belief we have not yet shifted from our minds.

Having already witnessed the splendid, luminous truth, these slips - back into lies - can be horribly distressing. Yet we know the pain will pass, so we sit back - doing what we can to cushion these inevitable falls - and go through again. It can be agonizing to be consciously aware of this world of the liar; this is reasonable and fair. Yet, here we are, right now. And even though we know there is a truly peaceful life for everyone; and even though the world is currently nothing like that place of beauty; there is a lot of work to be done and we'd better get on with it.

Suicide may seem like a good idea at times and for so many has been the only option for escaping the pain of an intolerable human existence. However, suicide is just another false promise coming from the liar in the mind. There is no escape in suicide. Destroying the body does not destroy the mind. When a person has reached an intensely desperate state of mind, suicide will only appear reasonable if they believe they are a body alone and that, therefore, the destruction of the body will mean the end of their suffering too. There is something circular here because the belief that we are only bodies underpins all our depression and isolation, so perhaps we could step back a moment and ask ourselves if we might be something more than just a body. Moreover, if we are just a body, then why would our thoughts matter at all?

If the mind is in pain - suffering guilt, envy, regret, hate, whatever it is - why do we assume that this can be eradicated by destroying the body? We have all had the experience of being in a dreadful mood and then suddenly, for no apparent reason, we are cheerful again. We didn't have to destroy a part of our body to achieve that; put simply a readjustment of thought took place. Furthermore, the only way we have ever been able to resolve a problem is by changing our minds about it. Changing our minds about a lie we have believed by discarding it for good, brings great relief and relaxation. However, until we change our minds, we suffer misery, stress, illness, and death - sadly, sometimes at our own hands.

What happens to consciousness when the body is destroyed is not for us to say here but we can reasonably suggest that the consciousness we share is not dependent on the body for its upkeep. Regardless of whether this idea is true or not, the belief that there is nothing more after the death of the body is terrifying. However, the liar loves this idea and has persuaded us to support it and use it to justify all sorts of arrogant and destructive actions; as if the most evolved form of life on the planet would reasonably produce as much chaos and ruin as it can in its short lifetime. When we believe that all life shares consciousness, if our little share of it is in turmoil, it is reasonable to assume that this little share will remain in turmoil, away from the body, until time passes and a readjustment takes place. Whatever the situation, the liar's promise of peace through death and suicide is false.

We must do our personal, as well as our collective, perceptual healing work. We are a very sick species right now, at the brink of self-annihilation; again, most likely. Healing can be sudden - remember, it has taken less than half a century for us to change our minds on homosexuality. Nevertheless, the approach to taking that first breath of truth can be tricky. Gaining an understanding of what it means to be human, and so discarding our dishonest past and reaching a state of peace, tranquillity, and joy - together with a strong sense of meaningfulness in our lives - will never be achieved by destroying the body. Destroying our own body is time wasting. And that is all it is.

You might wonder why, as with homosexuality, we are even bothering to forgive suicide. Well, for some it is a seriously bad thing to do. This idea mostly comes from undisputed religious beliefs. Amazingly, the liar has not only managed to lead us into horrors from which the only option for escape is to kill ourselves but, after having done so, it ensures that we remain doomed in the afterlife and in the minds of our fellows; a triple-whammy for the liar. It is absurd that we have managed to miss all this obvious madness, instead giving these lies extreme importance and causing so many, so much unnecessary pain when, in truth, all of it is nothing at all. Just lies. It is such a relief to find out.

No matter how bad it feels, we must see through the lies in order to uncover Heaven.com and the peaceful truth behind the shadows, and make our way safely to joyfulness. No matter how hard, fast, and deep the pain is, we must face it and examine it so that we might reveal it as the nonsense it is. If we do not look, we will never be sure of its falseness and it will always have some power over us. The examination of lies, itself, is easy. The approach to the examination is where the liar will be screaming blue murder at us, in order that we turn back from doing that which will surely leave it jobless.

However, if the agony of human existence becomes so intense we eventually end up destroying our own bodies in an attempt to alleviate our suffering; what then? Firstly, we should not worry or cause ourselves any more suffering. We should know that destroying the body cannot bring peace and the pain may well continue until we get another chance to resolve it. But we must know too that all this is OK and we are not to condemn anyone that chooses suicide for salvation, albeit in error. And I trust that those that do opt for this course of action are looked after.

Everything we do that does not come from loving thoughts is a kind of suicide; and practically everything we do does not come from loving thoughts. The human species, currently, is about to commit hara-kiri, albeit unwittingly; the self-destructive forces set in motion by the insane element in our thought-processes of which we are still unaware. The liar has been very successful in achieving its sick, psychotic goals; now even threatening our very home, that which sustains us. The truth can be shocking when we take a moment to look at it, carefully and dispassionately.

Thankfully, the beliefs that compel us to act destructively - in a bizarre attempt to save ourselves from our own fearfulness - are all lies, every single one. Yet while we believe them, they cause us much distress, and this belief, that we are bodies bound to die, is the worst of them all. Why not change our minds and believe something else instead, just to see what happens? I can assure you, it is a marvellous experience. What used to be, for me, a continuous daily hell, filled with fear and conflict in every thought (seen more clearly in retrospect) is now an indescribably joyful life, so peaceful and relaxed in comparison. I realise that every painful thought and experience I have ever had served to get me here. Thus, ironically, I am immensely grateful for every instant of it. Nevertheless, I would rather no-one had to repeat my experience, anywhere, ever.

Arriving at the state of mind in which I am able to write this book has been something like suicide, but only in terms of wittingly and consciously killing - by unravelling into nothing - the little liar-self that thinks it rules the whole universe, controlling everything, but doesn't in fact exist. Oh happy job that continues! And even though human beings under the liar's dictatorship believe we are the end goal, the winner, the pinnacle of life on Earth, it turns out that - no matter how hard we try and no matter what we believe - we cannot stop this relentless loving process of evolution, that which pulls us ever closer to union and Perfection.

11 GENOCIDE

Genocide is another horrible, yet logical, end result of the liar's work inside our minds. It is the extension of its original *very bad idea* into a sickening worst case scenario for humans - best case scenario for the liar - and just one step short of its real goal of the total annihilation of everything and everyone; the achievement which would finally - apparently - prove its sole dominion of the universe.

Genocide is likely the least disputable evidence we have of the liar's existence; in which the fact that the liar is not us, and its ideas not our own, can be most easily seen and accepted. We only have to take a quick look at the historical record to reveal the ghastly evidence of our madness taking the form of genocide all over the world; a stark warning, of the most gruesome variety, that our minds are not our own. However, even as we look at the numerous examples of genocide - and we cannot deny the insanity of humans - we still imagine the chaos is nothing to do with us personally. We remain steadfastly better-than those less-than humans. The truly insane are never aware of their insanity.

We make an extra effort to protect the liar's ideas in areas of our perception we cannot imagine doing without, regardless of the carnage such thinking might wreak. For example, we may argue ferociously that there is nothing at all amiss with how men and women define each other and themselves. We might become angry and defiant against the idea that we can no longer label *evil* those monsters we love to hate. To the clear-minded, the madness we are suffering is obvious, needing no defence at all, as none of it has any value worth protecting. However, a clear mind is something we need to work at and, until we achieve it, we will support the most insane ideas, without realising that we are doing so; even going as far as the justification of genocide.

Genocide, like paedophilia, is totally unjustifiable to a sane mind. Yet humans, in certain situations, have little trouble justify it. It is another extreme application of the same separated state of mind that enrages toddlers, forcing them into attacking each other at nursery school. To suggest a problem like this can be solved without first attempting to heal our collective insanity is part of the same separation psychosis that promotes it in the first place.

Defence and justification of the extinction of whole populations is left to those doing it, and only while it is being done. Somehow, we are able to justify such acts while in the thick of them. We may not understand how such justification can occur, but there is no real difference here to the justification of any type of violence against our fellows; even when it is the quietest, most bitter thought of hatred, said only to ourselves: *I wish you were dead*. It is all the same. The only real difference is in the present circumstances and the opportunities we have at hand for expressing our dark wishes; opportunities which, on occasion, permit us to live out our fantasies in the eradication of whole groups of people.

Genocide has been one of our most spectacular liar indulgences over the years. It happens somewhere far away and we are appalled and start pointing fingers. The doers, after the fact, are deeply ashamed. The instances of it get more gruesome and nightmarish each time. The rest of the world becomes enraged; seeking painful deaths, violent destruction and punishment of the *evil* ones. We talk, meet, talk and meet some more, and pass laws. There's a brief lull and then we do it all over again.

From the distant past there are countless examples, evidenced by ancient texts or historical and archaeological studies, of whole nations being wiped out by another group of people; people who were defined and labelled in a different way. Our more recent past and present are bloodier still. The definitions delineating different enough to murder are limitless; from odd religious practices, to speaking different languages, to height differences, to skin colour, to whether a person wears glasses or not, to having control of a cherished resource, or to living in a particular space believed to belong to the others, among many more.

Well, this is so obviously the work of the liar and more undeniable proof of human insanity. However, we continue to insist on the blame lying at someone else's door due to some intricate, debatable, and deconstructed part of the complicated analysis of why such a thing happened; about which we never are never clear; the liar's obfuscation indeed. As if murdering millions wasn't clear enough. But, sadly, misinterpreting the problem is the same as taking part in it; because our minds are controlled by a voice that detests peace and equality, or even a hint of them. Thus genocide is someone else's problem, until it arrives at our door; and until it does, those involved in it are less than us, in every sense. It is as absurd as those minor niggling complaints we have about other people, while not seeing the same behaviour so apparent in ourselves.

We justify past wars and genocide by maintaining our separation from the events and assuming a cold and emotionless witnessing of times gone by. We talk about men like Genghis Khan in a manner in which the bloody nature of their daily business is downplayed and diluted. We indulge ourselves excitedly in TV mini-series about the most brutal and murderous of royals. Will we be thinking about Hitler in the same way, 100 years from now? Perhaps there will be a BBC special about his life that ignores the pain of his victims and gives him a super-sick label of warring hero. We do that you know. Don't skip over the fact that our little boys playing cowboys and Indians are re-enacting genocide over and over; an example of our complicity in all human lunacy, so crystal clear if we would dare accept it.

Another key thing we must mention about the liar's form of forgiveness - that which delivers punishment and an eternity of condemnation - is that it must ensure the acts requiring forgiveness repeat themselves. This is the deal. The liar's forgiveness keeps its activities safe and protected, business as usual; and we should not forget that the liar will never be satiated until we destroy ourselves outright. If it is able to persuade us - after time has covered the horrors over in the foggy mist of loveless scholarship - that those having reached the highest levels of success in the destruction game are worth admiring, reading about, and re-enacting their atrocities as play, it's just doing its job, right?

Over the last 500 years or so we have committed genocide in epic proportions. If there are people to kill, we'll kill them. From the decimation of the indigenous peoples of the Americas, to the elimination of the Australian aboriginals, to the multi-holocausts of African nations, to the ethnic cleansing of populations, no part of the world is without a mention. Then, around 1914, we really got going, our passion for slaughter not dissipating, even after the writing of an international law against genocide in 1948, not that laws have ever done anything to stop crime, but they do allow us to punish them and so keep the liar's well-oiled wheel turning.

We like to think of ourselves as good and kind and reasonable. We tend to have high opinions of ourselves. We find comfort in our superiority, assured that our lives are exactly as they should be; quick to point to someone who isn't playing the game properly. Yet if we're so good, so kind, so superior, why did 160 million people die in wars in the last century? Our hands are extremely bloody and, just because you or I didn't actually pull the trigger, does not mean we are not close to someone who did or wouldn't also *just be doing our job* in the same situation. From the liar's perspective, if there is any opportunity for mass murder, the arguments supporting it will enter the group perception thick and fast. So far, there have simply not been enough of us on the side of sanity to have a counter effect on these senseless lies.

It is difficult to admit our failings, personally and from within the groups to which we belong. Children are often told they are wrong but they more easily assimilate failure, bouncing back quickly. As we get older, the liar sets like cement in our minds and, from here, the idea that we might be wrong can generate a level of fear in our minds that is so intense we might reasonably ask if it is any less than our fear of dying. This fear of being wrong causes us great discomfort personally and has also fuelled the most abominable acts of violence against our fellows.

We arrogantly believe we are the kings of the universe. We arrogantly believe our technology is supreme and worthy, when it is mostly just distraction. We arrogantly believe that chasing after tiny particles is of huge importance and worth the many billions spent on it. And while we're feeling so pleased with ourselves, we manage to avoid looking at the mass murder going on constantly, nearby and far away, as if it doesn't happen, as if it is some other species' problem.

We are proud of our heritage and our countries, yet we forget that the hands of our ancestors are dripping in blood. We are proud of our football teams and our flags, but we forget our wealth and comfort was built on the backs of slaves. We talk about our grandfather's elevated position in the military as if it were something of high value. The ability to wash over the mass murder occurring at that time - as if it hadn't happened - with the more important information on our high-ranking family members who took part in the conflict is remarkable; but the liar has never known any remorse for its actions.

We are very pleased with ourselves indeed, here in the West and elsewhere in the world. We believe we are doing so well, us humans, after a century of immense bloodshed. We forget we are all nearly homeless, our food and water is poison, the most wealthy of us spend our last years suffering a variety of horrific illnesses, over half of us are too scared to walk alone after dark, and our children are very insane.

Ironically, we reach old age and die horribly prolonged deaths in lonely hospital wards after enduring years of check-ups and unnecessary surgical procedures, each day ingesting fistfuls of pills sold by drug companies set up under the liar's goal of profit over all other considerations. Amazingly, genocide has now taken more sophisticated and indirect forms, where we may now be murdered stealthily in our beds instead of violently at each other's hands. The liar will use whatever opportunity is available towards its one grim goal of total destruction, don't doubt it for a second.

Ultimately we must see that humans share everything, both our healing and our sickness in all its forms. We have done our personal work and noticed that everything *bad* that happens to us is a reflection of our own state of mind. The next step is to extrapolate that into the collective consciousness. If I notice myself having destructive thoughts, the idea that *it is only me having them* is the liar's separating business again. We will share peace, but right now we are sharing war. And we are not alone in our madness.

We might say that the only truth is love, and this would be correct, but while most of us have no idea what love is - confusing it with sex, apathy, and other baloney - what better thing to do than to look at how our belief in hatred does not stand up to scrutiny. What better thing to do than to look at *not-love* and disprove its reality. We will see that our minds are very sick and need immediate attention.

Step one in any addiction program is admitting there is a problem. When we cannot admit there is a problem, nothing can be done about it. It is impossible to have an effect on something we don't believe exists. Yet we are all addicted to the liar's voice, without exception. Even when we are aware of the lies and illusion, we are still here so we still believe them in some sense. Denying our obvious problem is most unhelpful and a particularly devious liar device. While we avoid facing our problems head on, we will never find a way out of them. If we continue to deny the obvious, we will leave peace of mind to a handful of sane humans. The pragmatic acceptance of genocide, and all liar-based activities, as simply the logical end products of a sick human mind - from which we all are suffering - will be the beginning of an effective remedy to that over which we have been puzzling forever.

The importance we give something delineates how much control it has over us. We certainly give a lot of importance to war, violence, and death, albeit mostly in a voyeuristic manner. But who or what could have successfully persuaded us that any of this is of interest at all? Are we that enraptured with pain and suffering, viciously willing to defend it, or are we just living out the projected fantasies of the liar in our minds? We all share exposure to genocide, whether we experience it for real by being the button-presser, trigger-puller, or machete-swinger, or whether we just whoop inside every night at the killings, fake and genuine, we see on TV.

Over time, the machinery of murder has become more intricate, technologically advanced, and disconnected from the pain of its victims. Human evolution, as the liar has it, is dependent on getting closer to the point of destroying ourselves completely. Each occurrence of genocide complies with the liar's sick definition of evolution by successfully killing greater numbers with greater ease. Furthermore, the more clinical, cold, and heartless we can be in murdering our brothers - who have become non-human nothings in our perception - the more medals we receive from our earthly superiors.

The fearful fantasies and stories we tell reveal our unchecked assumption that more highly evolved beings would have to have perfected the destruction we believe is a measure of success. The tales of technologically advanced, external *evil* beings, terrorising and attacking us from beyond, are the projections of this belief we never question. But what if we stopped a moment to look at this mad idea we all accept wholeheartedly? It is clearly nonsensical rubbish. We don't even know we believe it, but we do. No other species is hell bent on destroying itself. Why would the great and mighty human being be dead set on nothing else?

We have probably been here a very long time as humans. The difference between us and our nearest neighbours, in an evolutionary sense, is enormous. We are nowhere near to the finished product, yet somehow we have managed to live relatively peacefully in our current human state for long periods of time. The liar functions as a perceptual bridge from older states of fear to the new fearless consciousness we are now at the point of reaching. However, this liar, albeit seemingly necessary in some sense, is also a weapon of mass self-destruction. Since we got organised and technological, the liar has really got moving; and one of its key functions is avoiding discovery. It does this very well, as we sleepily forget the most recent genocide and the suffering of millions.

The increasing rate and occurrence of genocide in the last 500 years has left us culturally bereft. The beauty and wonder we have lost, destroyed, stamped, out and deleted from the human world is staggering; reflected by the daily extinction of non-human species (speciocide?). And, if we're honest, we don't really care either. Traditional peoples may well have fear as a reliable partner in their lives too, but their ways are conjoined with the environment and there is interconnectedness, respect, and balance between human activity and the natural world; a balance of which our modern life has no notion.

In the past, human life functioned reasonably well; existing side-by-side with nature, not taking too much and giving back as much as was taken. Humans maintained a balance with the environment and perceptual world views of ancient hunter-gatherers compare favourably with the most effective of modern psychotherapies, and are still more efficacious in dealing with disease and depression. However, due to our over-inflated view of ourselves, and the much supported lack of importance of other living things, the inevitable has happened. That which we believe deserves no intrinsic respect or consideration is being irrevocably ruined. We miss the fact that what we are destroying is our home, and so too our life force. Perhaps we could fantasise about colonising Mars; now that would solve the problem surely! The mess we are in is of astronomical proportions, and only the liar can distract us from it. But the liar is not us.

There is a state of mind that may relate to human behaviour like that of Hitler and Pol Pot in the same way we all now relate to the behaviour of gorillas. This is the forgiven mind. Although we have most certainly brought the fear of previous stages of evolution into our experience, certain things from older times we have decidedly stopped without a second thought. The act of genocide, in our future free-minded state, will have the same unlikelihood of occurrence as humans today copying the behaviour of the higher primates who have not yet learned that faeces are not an ideal dinner. There is much more to the Buddhist concept of monkey mind than meets the eye.

If, by looking at genocide and its supporting foundations, we may more easily see the liar's activities, then even genocide can have its key part to play in the collective healing we so desperately need. We may use the dark shadows to serve the light of knowledge, peace, and freedom so that no-one will have suffered in vain in some sense.

When we know what the liar in our perception is, we will have to admit that genocide is not only inevitable but will keep occurring until we manage to undo our belief in better-than-ness over others, that which needs constant defence. Moreover, looking at our insanity, even just once, properly, with open eyes, never to misunderstand the problem again, ensures forgiveness for our brothers for the genocide they can justify, and our sisters for going along with them.

12 THE ATLANTIC SLAVE TRADE

And if we needed yet another glaring proof of our insanity, here it is.

There is something big lacking in our lives. We all feel it; deep down, and not so deep down. We are sure this feeling of lack is real but we cannot put our finger on exactly what it is we lack. Instead, we attempt to replenish the lack with an endless stream of relationships, distractions, and addictions, but nothing seems to suffice. It is this deep sense of lack - coupled with the surety of being isolated and alone in our skins - that drives the ferocious pursuit of distractions which we mistakenly believe will heal our pain, or at least stop us being conscious of it. We may amass such distractions in vast numbers.

The more we have of something we consider valuable, the surer we are of our own better-ness, our winning state when compared to our fellows. But all this is just another liar defence, because there can never be a winner as we are all equal. Competition between equals is an oxymoron. Thus, the liar's activities of amassing and claiming ownership of apparently valuable items in order to win a perceptual competition in which we are all taking part are illogical, frenetic, and unstable at the very best. We have even invented a symbolic representation of value, in order to show off to the world how many of the distractions we own; money, of course, which makes the liar's business of ownership and reciprocity far simpler in practice.

From the position of better than the rest - that which needs constant defence because it will never be true - one can barely perceive the mind's slip into justifying destructive activities that promise to generate more better-than, particularly when such better-than takes the form of profit. Profit is our God and we will do just about anything to serve it. The liar promises that, by destroying our brothers and taking what they have, we will be better than they are, and that this is our only worthy goal. When the liar insists upon the relentless pursuit of profit above all other considerations and, furthermore, to use as the commodity itself large numbers of human beings with no right to humanness, we are looking again at the inevitable insanity of human thinking, that which we *all* share, without exception.

Becoming clear minded about our behaviour can be tiring and depressing. We don't want to do the work of looking at ourselves because, deep down, we know what we will see. What we humans do, without knowing why or how we could, is so ghastly, so unbelievable, it is little wonder we would rather hide beneath the duvet with a special other, get drunk and high, or fill our minds with unrelenting fantasies. Yet what we have to gain by looking is freedom, nothing less; freedom from a species-wide mental slavery in which we all choose to remain due to ignorance. However, we can make another choice, at any moment.

Once enough of us have understood and undone the madness, the children arriving on Earth will inherit a perception in which the objectification of another human being for personal gain, in any sense, is preposterous. The smoking addict defiantly argues that he enjoys smoking and has no intention of stopping; we all know he's lying, and mostly to himself. Anyone that insists on keeping liar ideas intact in the human perception will be like the defiant smoker that prefers to kill himself instead of facing the truth. Life without nicotine addiction is available to us at any moment, as is a loving and peaceful human perception. Furthermore, that is what we want - all of us - no matter how much we think we don't, or kick and scream against it.

The road to clarity seems heavy at times; particularly as, along the way, we must start to notice our own complicity in the perceptual problem shared by all humanity. After initial feelings of doom and depression, as we strip our false superiority away, we realise that something very wonderful is happening. Healing takes place and suddenly, for the first time in our lives, we notice we have some control over our thoughts and emotions; they are not totally running our lives anymore. From here, we can witness our thoughts, watching carefully for the liar. We can pick out its ideas clearly, throwing them away for good, while holding onto anything representing love and unity.

It is one thing doing our own personal work but, as we take the work to the collective consciousness, we can become despondent again. The task ahead seems so enormous. We need to be clear and so few of us are. Here we must rely on faith, remembering our own success in changing our personal lives around from a relentless hell to joy. We remember, too, the past proofs of our collective forgiveness potential and the ability we have to change our group perception nearly instantaneously, with little repercussion.

This is very important. It is like what happened when we figured out that the earth is a planet and so round, not flat. Overnight, practically, we shifted our perception in a previously unimaginable way. In a very short time, this new realisation completely rewrote our world-view and has shaped our experience ever since. From this single scientific discovery came technological advances once considered outlandish dreams. Let's do the same now, by finally noticing something of staggering importance to humans. Let's see, and so discard, this thing that controls our lives, leading us ever more steadily towards devastation of unbelievable proportions. Collective human freedom is possible. It has to be. However, each of us must be sure of exactly what we are ditching, because the liar in our minds will shout and scream and caterwaul that it is an essential part of our lives and should remain.

I feel like I've proved the thesis - the existence of the liar in the mind - countless times already. Yet we still have work to do because there are outstanding events for which we would likely save a belief in *evil* if we do not look at them with new eyes. The slave trade of Africans to the Americas is one of the most shocking atrocities committed by humans against humans that we continue to have difficulty forgiving.

Interestingly, we understand the foundations of the slave trade because we are all running the race of financial better-than and worse-than. We all define ourselves by our relative wealth or poverty, so to explain how such a thing could have got going is not too difficult. What is more difficult to forgive is the subsequent division into worse-than and better-than of the human owners and the human owned, utilising the obvious skin colour contrast as a basis for, and proof of, separateness and so inequality. The racism alone kept the slave trade - along with all its horrors - delivering the dollars. Moreover, forgiveness of the racism remains outstanding in the collective consciousness today.

It is nearly inconceivable that one human being could subject another to kidnap, imprisonment, beatings, whippings, wanton punishment, rape, murder, enforced pregnancies, work without pay, denigrations, and a whole host of daily outrages, for no other reason than that the human was a commodity, belonging to another person by law. The liar in the human mind reveals itself here when we notice that we don't treat our machinery, now doing the same work, in the same way. How can we understand, and so forgive, such barbarity? The task seems impossible indeed; but try we must, for peace of mind and freedom from the species-wide slavery we are all enduring.

We project the guilt generated by even a tiny act of hatred towards any brother or sister by an insistence on their worse-than-ness.

Projecting our guilt onto our victims is supposed to relieve ourselves of it. Thus, proving the worse-than-ness of victims, and so justifying our bestial behaviour, *requires* harsh treatment. We had to brutalise the Africans in slavery in the Americas in order to mitigate the guilt that arose from assuming them non-human. It was an inevitable and logical step for the liar in our minds and the process is not limited to these events.

Harsh actions against our fellows naturally generate profound levels of guilt in our hearts. Being one species, we are, in truth, treating *ourselves* in the same way we treat our brothers. All this is pain to an already insane mind, which the liar quickly persuades into inflicting more intense harsh actions which it promises are an escape from the pain of guilt. Even when *crimes* based on misidentifying a human being with something less-than-human are legal - such as any objectification of a person - the instigators suffer guilt.

Objectification, a particularly common form our insanity takes, is difficult to see when applied to our best friend, but easy to see in the actions of slave owners of all varieties, and it is exactly the same thing. Whatever the intensity and effects of our actions, and whatever we believe, we will never mitigate our guilt with more harshness and brutality. However, slave owners believe this false promise coming from the liar in the human mind and, inevitably, during the Atlantic slave trade, the madness, punishment, and destruction spiralled out of control. We are still feeling the repercussions of the hatred generated by the need to justify the unthinkable towards millions of human beings.

Only the liar could have invented slavery. The liar's voice tells us that certain humans, arbitrarily picked out as not the same as us - usually by a significant physical difference - are less-than human. We have little difficulty believing they are non-human. This belief is obviously not true and it is therefore an easy next step into treating these people badly in order to attempt to prove and justify their less-than state. Belief in lies is the only way we are able to abuse other people, be it our best friend, our spouse, or millions of people labelled in a particular derogatory way.

This is going on everywhere we look. A person paying for sex rents another human body - an object - for a short time; and he will not escape the guilt of having dehumanised his fellow human in this way. Barefoot workers in China, earning a pittance in order to make fortunes for wealthy corporations selling us our mobile phones, are treated like dogs; and their bosses will not know peace of mind. Little children working without pay - on fear of death if they disagree - in order to supply rich yuppies in the West with their distracting substances and barely memorable nights out; and the criminal farmers will be living in self-made hells. Everywhere we look, we see humans treating other humans as less-than human and suffering the inevitable consequences. By understanding the liar-mind model of perception to which we are all willing and ignorant subjects, we must see that the horrors arising from the insanity it causes are inevitable.

Like the crucifixion of Christ and the attempted extinction of the Jewish people in the Second World War, the slave trade is another extreme example of what can happen when the liar in our minds becomes completely out of control. We are not wholly insane, however. We occasionally become so outraged at unacceptable behaviour, we do try and stop it; especially when it gets so barbaric we are unable to look the other way any longer. Sadly, our solutions to our problem usually include some blood-shedding. Yet we are still in the liar's world and so we only have the liar's solutions in any case. There has been no other way to deal with incidents like the slavery of millions, up until now.

The slave trade required, and so generated, proof of the belief that non-white people were of little value when compared to white people. The slave trade itself did not start on this racist basis; the slaves taken to the Americas had been sold to European slavers by Africans who had originally kidnapped them. Over four centuries, African slaves spent their lives in chains, working themselves into the grave in order to build the wealth of Europe and North America. Before the slave trade, there had been little contact between white Europeans and black Africans and so hatred based on skin colour differences is not apparent in the historical record. However, from the beginning of the Atlantic slave trade, a vile hatred towards black people started to form, grow, and flourish; a necessary part of projecting the guilt away from the perpetrators and onto the victims.

This hatred took some extraordinary forms under the guise of scientific facts - we will see more of this grotesque thinking when we look at Nazi ideas later on. Among a plethora of insane activities, academic studies were undertaken, in all seriousness, to prove that the black African was non-human. This would be a most useful result for those treating these human beings like farm animals for profit and, even though we could never prove such nonsense, the ideas stuck and permeated through communities, populations, and continents; the hatred incited by them still reasonable to some minds today.

Four centuries of projected guilt in the form of continued violence, aggression, and depraved treatment towards innocent human beings; constant belittlement, humiliation, and denigration and the successful application of a label of non-human that needed constant brutal reinforcement; millions upon millions of people uprooted from their homeland and taken into enforced servitude in a strange place with unfamiliar languages and customs; millions more born into this hell, to spend their whole lives in it. This is our human legacy. This is what we have to show the generations to come of what we are capable with our minds under dictatorship. And this is how all of us may behave when we listen to the liar's voice and follow its advice, without knowing that we do.

What we tell ourselves becomes true for us. Our thoughts dictate our life experiences. If we are born into a particular culture, we take on its characteristics. If our parents drink and smoke to excess, we will probably do the same. If our culture demands we marry and have children, we will most likely do so. If our surroundings are detrimental to our health in any way, it will take a brave and conscious effort to avoid considering such environments as normal. Moreover, it will take even more courage to avoid passing them off as normal to our offspring. Those who are told, constantly, by their parents, teachers, guardians, or peers that they are worthless and no good, will struggle to break free of these shackling ideas.

The resulting conclusions of the persistent negative labelling of black people were believed whole-heartedly by everyone involved, including the Africans themselves. This proves how powerful our minds are. Whatever we believe takes form in the world somehow, even when it is a total lie. We are twisted sorcerers, all of us, and by our own sick thinking, we projected the mental slavery we suffer out into the world to wreak as much havoc as it could, just as the liar demands.

The slave trade's legacy reaches much further than we can possibly imagine. Not only does fiercely irrational violence and hatred continue across the world, based upon the same imaginary principles, but whoever we are, we still see this form of separation psychosis by the words, pictures, and ideas we witness in the common collective consciousness. The media continues to reinforce the negative beliefs imprinted in our minds over many centuries.

Humans whose ancestors spent their lives in slavery will undoubtedly carry inherited remnants of the pain and suffering that their forefathers endured until we are able to heal our minds properly. Furthermore, this healing must be collective work; and not selectively collective either or we risk inviting the liar into the proceedings and so the eternal wheel of destruction will roll happily on.

Only the liar trivialises pain; most successfully in the media pastimes with which we choose to indulge ourselves; but this is not our indulgence here. If we maintain any belief in an inherent evilness, or worse-than-ness, of anyone defined by a physical difference, we have done nothing to change the record. Instead, just like women might be the violent ones in the centuries to come if we fail to rid ourselves of the liar in our minds - the definition of success remaining the measure of how destructive we can be - so too might the descendants of African slaves become the bitter wealthy slave holders of the future. There is no solution in separation, in cherishing and protecting our personal pain. Nothing is ever resolved under the liar's dictatorship where differences reign supreme, whatever they might be. Whenever we confine someone, anyone, to the flames of hell for all eternity in our minds, we go right along there with them.

Suffering is non-discriminative and no-one has a monopoly on violence. The liar's whim can change in an instant - previous *victims* becoming present *oppressors*. Let's not get caught up in finger pointing and labelling without first knowing that it is only the liar who finger points, maintaining separation at all costs, even when we believe we are righteously entitled to *own* our ghastly story. Owning suffering keeps it intact, perceptually away from sharing and so healing. It maintains that one person's suffering is more important than another's; the liar's persuasion. Furthermore, nothing we have done yet has stopped humans justifying this form of profiteering across the world. Today's estimate is nearly 30 million people in slavery.

Suffering is, obviously, not a competition, but the liar will persuade us that it is. Separation psychosis, ironically, knows no boundaries, and if we cannot share responsibility for all the activity of the liar - regardless of whether we had a personal hand in it or not - then separation is maintained and the world is doomed. We share everything, our pain and our joy. Our joy is the choice we make with a free will, while our pain is a ready-meal, handed to us on plate without forethought. In truth, our fingers can point to one thing only, the liar. When we know that the liar's ideas will never define us, we become aware that peace is a realistic option for all. We begin to experience this personally in our daily lives. Soon it becomes clear that if there is anyone - even just a single person - suffering in the world, then we are not yet free.

If I can admit that under a certain set of circumstances, in a certain time period, given a particular body form and gender, I too would have been at the dishing out end of atrocities such as those committed during the Atlantic slave trade, then I know for sure that there is no-one in the universe any better or worse than myself. Even when our part is just apathy and tacit approval, we should be aware of our responsibility, while recognising that the problem is in human thinking alone. Our faulty thinking is an error we can fix. And that's all there is to the liar. It is not, in fact, racist or sexist. It just needs to persuade us that those separating ideas are worth protecting. It does a good job too, in an arbitrary, non-committal, utterly merciless manner. We eventually made the right decision about the Atlantic slave trade. We can do so with the origin of the problem too.

The better-thans of old become the worse-thans of today. We all live by the same standard of better-than; only the actors and locations seem to swap roles and labels, shifting and changing, century by century. There is always better-than and worse-than with the liar in our mind, although better-than never delivers its promised gifts. We may find ourselves at the top of the heap yet miserable, frustrated, and angry; perhaps worse off emotionally than we ever were as *victim* and worse-than. Maybe that's where we are right now; suffering the effects of another false promise believed. There is only suffering under the liar's ideas, whether we are better or worse, or whatever.

In a world in which profit over all other considerations is king, the profiting is always based upon the liar's foundation of inequality. The liar understands our deep lacking very well, knowing exactly what it is we unconsciously feel we are missing. It will never let us see the truth of this, however, and instead offers us limitless substitutions that, it says, will address this need, replenish our lack, and bring us peace of mind. We chase after these substitutions like a mass of ghoulish heroin addicts after their next fix. From a new car, to a new husband, to the subjugation of millions of people, none of the liar's substitutions have ever given us what we want, and yet we are compelled to seek more of the same. It is, of course, unutterably insane, and everything we do in the world functions under these false assumptions.

When we perceive the world from within the shrieking of the liar's temptations to conflict, all human problems remain external to us, nothing to do with us personally; to be solved by some other, some miracle worker maybe. This is the liar's idea again, because we all must do our bit. Looking at the result of the liar's activities in the world shows us that it is truly winning this game of lies and truth, war and peace. The slave trade is an extreme example of what we all do when we take advantage of a fellow human being. We must paint her black in order we might justify our own nauseous behaviour towards her.

As humans, we are conscious beings and it is our consciousness alone that defines our experience of the world. In our current state of unawareness, we can but project our fears onto the world around us and everyone in it. While dozing, we do not question our use of words, the ideas we consider reasonable, or our thoughts about other people. Even slavery can appear legitimate, as our urge to profit overtakes any other sane thought to the contrary. The truth is that slavery is a projection of every human being's state of mind. We are all prisoners inside a perceptual prison and, mostly, we have no idea that this is so.

Waking up is a process of recognising our surroundings, seeing that the nature of our lives is dependent on conflict and hatred, and dismantling all the beliefs that persuade us to act violently and unethically. What we have to gain by understanding the liar is freedom, nothing less. Becoming aware of the liar's activities, and so beginning the process of discarding it, will bring us the freedom from mental slavery that, in truth, we crave.

Just like the severely clinically insane remain unaware of their own insanity, the human species remains unaware of its profound separation psychosis. However, as we heal our minds, we will become certain of our togetherness, equality, and connection. When the idea of separation is totally unreasonable, there will be no option but to recognise that we would behave exactly the same way as our brothers, given their state of mind and circumstances. Each time we look carefully and calmly at the liar's actions, assured of our equality, we generate yet another projection; but this time a loving one, a unified perception, the alarm clock of our consciousness ringing: *Time to wake up!*

13 THE MEDIA

We probably used to learn about who was worse and who was better from our families, relatives, and the people of our small tribe or the village in which we lived. We probably used to spend whole afternoons discussing what the woman living down by the inn - her with the *past* - had worn to mass the day before. We probably used to tut-tut as she passed us on her way to the farm. We'd feel better than her for sure; and what a relief. We might even feel some delicious self-importance if we were the one telling the stories about her for the first time Perhaps we were, now and then, persuaded to embellish and invent in order to please our audience and claim even more accolade.

As our villages grew into towns and cities, our useless information-sharing need grew at a similar rate. Thus, we invented the press, then radio, cinema, TV, and now Internet; together deemed a huge industry - the media. Unsurprisingly, these surrogate eyes of the world rarely paint a pretty picture of human life on earth. Today, instead of the garden fence, we have daytime TV in which there seems to be no limit to the depravity on show. Ignorance blooms and flourishes, supplying the desires of a finger-pointing audience. Pride is now evaluated on who can be the most depraved. The liar is functioning so efficiently in our world today, it has even persuaded us that better-than is achievable by the most self-destructive human behaviour - the worse, the better - an astonishing and appalling reversal of meaning.

The famous are undoubtedly better-than, regardless of what they have done to deserve it. Fame is another of the liar's lack-replenishing offerings. Even a previously peaceful mind may be persuaded into behaving outrageously due to the liar's promise of relief from isolation when filling up on the indisputably valuable commodity of fame. Fame satisfies our desire to live forever, somewhat illogically. It entices us with singing contests and reality TV shows, while the truly famous carry on their very important lives and relationships, each fart respectfully reported by the designated holy messengers of the rubbish we gorge upon and believe will save us.

You've got to hand it to the liar, managing to keep us completely distracted 24 hours a day, 365 days a year. We existed for many thousands of years, our minds fixed on daily survival alone. We worked like mules, living very short lives in order to feed our families and stay alive. Relatively few people enjoyed wealth until very recently; and comfort like we know it now would have previously been unimaginable for the masses. We fail to notice that with our current comfort comes a one-in-a-million opportunity to look at our minds and heal them. No, not today, sorry; we can't be bothered with that because we're far too busy finishing up the best-selling BDSM novel, or finding out who slept with who on the most inane of soap operas, or feverishly trying to break through level 65 on Candy Crush.

Having inherited the concept of *it's a hard life* without ever questioning the idea's validity, we have inevitably projected it into the drudge and boredom of our lives today, even though we are part of the many lucky millions who do not - in fact - have such a hard life anymore. But the belief that human life must be full of suffering is deeply embedded, even when we live in a wealthy country with all the basic necessities to hand. Nevertheless, we are convinced that life is awful and unpleasant, and goodness, we didn't ask to be born, so why not invent a million distractions to avoid looking at the condition of the world we live in and our true state of mind. Great idea!

It seems that we are distracting ourselves from the pain of our lives but, in fact, by not being honest with ourselves, we ensure that the pain continues. Even our tiny children are caught up in the liar's circular, convoluted, and destructive ideas as they take on its mantras of conflict from as early an age as possible. When we finally do turn away from the distractions, we are forced to look at what is in our minds. It is usually, initially, not a pretty sight. However, without being honest with ourselves, there is no hope of resolving our sadness and frustration. The liar knows this very well and commands forcefully: *Don't look!* and we obey.

Yes, what a great idea, let's become addicted to fantasy; that way we won't have to accept the horrors we dole out to each other and ourselves. The nightly news is hardly realistic anyway; dark-skinned poor people, a long way away, suffering awfully - oh, and is my programme on yet, on the other side? Click. When destruction arrives at our door, as it eventually always does, we will scream and wail and moan and point the finger at someone, but we won't resolve any of our problems by doing so. Better to watch TV, play computer games, or get high...yes, let's get high instead! Someone else can fix the world, maybe, perhaps not; oh well, we've just about destroyed it anyway, nothing to be done now, never mind, X-Factor's on; are there any beers in the fridge dear?

Getting clear means going into our past to see what's entwined there in perceptual chains and bolted together with lies. When we see what's there, we will finally understand our predicament. From here we can undo the locks and begin the long overdue healing of our minds. Once the big stuff is out of the way - that which will not give us peace until it is dealt with - the clearing of smaller personal matters continues and, on occasion, we are offered the opportunity of remembering something seemingly insignificant from the past, but seen with this new, clear vision. Recently, I received one of these memory gifts. I remembered being at school; a memory from when I was about 7 years old. I went back to those days and began to relive the games we used to play in the playground at break-times. What I saw was very interesting indeed.

When we were little girls, we played make-believe at school. We had all sorts of games, families, husbands and wives, boyfriend and girlfriends, things like that. We'd spend ages inventing the characters, naming them very precisely, and setting up their relationships. We'd spend even more time discussing the protagonists of the make-believe stories at length; whether they had children, what colour shoes they wore, and if they were tall or short. We talked a lot about how they looked. Then we'd spend yet more time describing how things were going to work in the game. There'd be a house that would look a certain way and one of us would live there. The others would come for tea. It would always be summer, of course, and someone would have to fly to America. Ages and ages of delightful story telling took place in setting up the game.

Then we were done inventing new fantasies and it was time to start the game. The game would begin. Within minutes, we got bored and drifted away, ending up doing something completely different instead. We did not notice anything bizarre about this and would repeat the whole process again the next day. When something is boring and not working, children pick up on it immediately and shift their attention, moving onto a more interesting thing. Kids are able to admit defeat - without admitting defeat. They just change their minds, and so its focus, and that's that.

The moral of the story is: the reality of what we fill our heads with is actually very dull! Children are able to see this instantaneously and try something else. The fact that, as children, we kept on trying to play the same boring game, over and over, shows our insanity was already pretty fixed. As adults, nothing much has changed. We accept that real life is dull and monotonous, so we use stories and fantasies to escape from it.

The TV shows, films, books, and computer games we indulge on are full of excitement, titillation, sex, violence, and glamour and we live vicariously through them. We know that real life can never be like the TV shows and, therefore, we assume that real life will never fulfil us. From this sad conclusion of the human experience, we are unable to take responsibility for anything that is happening in the world; we just don't care enough about it. The liar has managed to persuade us that sleep is preferable to waking so it can get on with its dastardly plan with no dissent, right in front of our noses. Its lullaby to us is the media.

I wonder how many of us imitate the excitement-generating activities portrayed in TV shows and trashy novels, just to spice up our boring lives. Like anything that the liar says is good to do, the results are guaranteed to be tremendously disappointing. But like our childhood games, perhaps we will keep on trying. I wonder how many of the regular, multi-million-odd viewers of a particular soap opera believe that normal people are as miserable, angry, frustrated, and spiteful as the characters they see on the show each night, those characters that feel like old friends. I wonder if anyone realises that wealthy better-thans are writing the scripts that describe the lives of poor people, the worse-thans, and so projecting onto them the misery they believe is a requirement for anyone who can't afford an IPhone, or whatever.

The liar cannot hide many of its ideas. We see them clearly in films, TV, books, paintings, and any artistic pursuit. Indeed, anything we project onto externally reveals our sick thinking. The body reigns supreme in the media, no surprises there. What we write in stories and fantasies is what is in our own minds, and the lowest self-esteem may sell a lot of books simply because we share the author's unrecognised low opinion of herself and are, therefore, desperate to indulge it. When we notice the amount of violence, aggression, anger, hatred, and heartless sex in what we see, night after night, we are simply witnessing the dreadfully unhealthy state of the collective human mind at the current time. Not only that, we approve of it, and feed it with our need for more gore, more intense violence, more cold violent fucking, and more chances to become famous or win our way out of hell.

Our stories are so wonderful. We kill the bad guys. Sometimes the bad guys are even cooler than the good guys. They certainly get to do a lot more violence. Perhaps we prefer the bad guys. How wonderful to be able to indulge our desire to be bad, to be a real badass criminal druggie, or a real hard-as-nails cop busting those badass criminal druggies; nothing like the bleak reality of these worlds at all. Even the drug scene gets a Hollywood gloss, making it appear special and enticing. Yet not so far away, under the veneer of drug-taking, women-owning, too-cool-for-school beliefs is deprivation, pain, and suffering. Nevertheless, drugs, violence, and voluminous amounts of sex are worthwhile pastimes as portrayed by the media. And we believe it, too. How cool it is to be bad these days, these days when bad means good and sick means really good! As if our madness wasn't clear enough already, we are screaming at ourselves to wake up and notice our errors.

TV and the media allow us to indulge the liar with no obvious repercussions. It gets its fix of devastation in the minds of our children, countless times a day. When children regularly witness - a daily event on the TV and one in which they delight - they will be mostly compliant when required for real killings further down the line. We are enured to murder, genocide, sex crimes, and the destruction of innocents in any form, and we just don't give a damn that our fellows sharing the planet with us are living in these hellish circumstances in actuality.

Can we honestly say that our minds are our own, or that we are completely sane, when we consider all this normal? We are buffeted around at the whim of advertisers; liking this, hating that, getting furious about a person's choices world's away, unaware of the pain our neighbour might be suffering, or caring very much at all about the state of things. Our children learn and copy the same destructive and apathetic tendencies, subtle or overt, accepting this ultra-violent world as it is without question; just as we do.

Do we reach our last days wishing we had done something different? Do we end up wishing we had made a difference, or at least tried to? Do we truly want to hand this madness down to our children's children?

The media doles out fear and humdrum, fear and humdrum, and precious little of the wonder that we are; although that is also there to see just as clearly, but only when we are looking properly. We unconsciously express the truth of human equality, love, and compassion in the media because these things are truly part of us and we cannot help but project what we are. Seeing these glimpses of the light, shining through the heavy curtain of the virus infested Heaven.com, are the first welcome signs that we have changed our direction, even if just a little. However, in our fierce denial of the light of truth, we don't need to have a real life, if there were any such thing. Witnessing continuous misery, violence, and sex each night on TV satiates the liar in our minds, keeping it highly activated and in total control. The following day at school and work, we will discuss all the horrors we saw with great fervour.

All the fantasies and stories we delight in are meaningless; even - yet more subtly of course - the high-brow documentaries. We don't think so however, otherwise we wouldn't bother with them. Furthermore, if any of it is of value, it follows that we must consider our lives to be extra-meaningless, as we are attempting to escape our lives by becoming obsessed with trash. It is no wonder sleep is preferable to real life, if real life (life without the liar) could be worse than our thoughts about it!

Like the most important person in the village, she who had access to the most information, getting a job in the media assures us of a god-like status. Our job may as well be taking buckets of toxic sludge into schools and spoon-feeding the children with the contents. Our contracts order constant reinforcement of toxic ideas, such as the unquestionable supreme ruler of the universe, the beautiful young body, without which a person is doomed. We learn from the media that white skin is better than dark skin; blatantly in countries where skin-whitening products make vast fortunes for the few, and subtly in the West where better-than roles are still white only. Furthermore, if you count the women to men ratio in the majority of films, plays and TV shows, you might reasonably assume that women don't contribute anything of any importance in the world, perhaps they don't even exist in some places!

We could be here all day making a list of the lies the media reinforces before we even approach the specific lies distributed at the request of whatever government might be in charge of a country's media at a particular time. Well, wouldn't do the same you if it was going to ensure and protect your better-than status? Yes, we would.

The media is the liar's shiny new toy we have gifted it, and how could we not have? With its cool new amusement, it is able to spread its message as far and as wide as possible. Nearly every idea the media supports and propounds is part of the liar's model of reality; and how could it be any other way given that the liar has total control of our minds?

We have made ourselves so comfortable - defending ourselves against the harsh reality of a world based on false principles - that, ironically, we now have the time to free our minds and so begin the only true work of saving the world. Discarding lie after lie reveals to us what is underneath this rubbish tip. Miraculously, we find love, compassion, togetherness, and equality under the madness. From a place of love it is nearly impossible to indulge ourselves like we used to. Like the nausea we feel when we think of that bad food item that made us horribly sick decades ago, the idea of spending a night in watching trash TV has the same appeal as drinking poison.

A loving environment, with little violence around, may be enough to support our children's immunity against the violent thinking that underpins our cultures. These are tentative first steps on the road to a more inclusive and collective healing. Undoing the liar in our minds brings us happiness and peace. We start to like ourselves and begin enjoying our own company, without distractions. The beneficial effects we have on others are obvious. When we stop distracting ourselves there is time for personal healing and there has not been a moment in history like this, ever before, in which many millions of us may free ourselves together. This is a golden opportunity. Let's take it.

In the meantime, we should understand that the media, as it is, is a warning. It portrays the vileness inside our minds and will remain the same until we heal ourselves. It is not to blame for anything by itself, as it is just an effect of our collective disease. The people working in the media, supporting the continued insanity and feeling good about themselves for doing so, have no idea about what is going on, so they are also not to blame for anything either. Again, as always, the finger points back at its origin. Only the liar is to blame, for anything.

14 THE DRUG TRADE

Little plant and her family have grown wild in the region for many millions of years. They have enjoyed a peaceful and happy existence for nearly all this time. In the past, little plant's ancestors were picked by humans from the nearest settlement and taken to the tribe who smoked them, or drunk them, or applied them to wounds, or ingested them as a key ingredient in a medicinal preparation. These humans came to little plant with a very important question that needed answering. Little plant and her family were always happy to help. Humans celebrated and petitioned little plant in rituals with drumming, music, and singing. Little plant and her family would help the tribe with their tricky question, providing a solution to the problem, and bringing peace to people, families, and small communities.

More recently, humans were carrying little plant off without asking any question. Little plant and her family found this very strange. When they looked at the place of questioning in the human being they saw many, many questions. But the human did not ask a single question nor perform any ritual. Little plant and her family thought about this for a long time, puzzling over what to do. In the end, they decided that it would be better if little plant and her family took control of such chaotic decision makers, rather than let them run loose with their unanswered questions. They reasoned that, eventually, the human would start asking the right questions and, when he did, little plant would help him.

Little plant and her family took control of the minds of the humans that asked no questions, in order to protect them from themselves. As well as taking control, little plant gave the human brief glimpses of a better way in the hope that one day he would start asking the right questions.

Even more recently, the numbers of humans that were coming to take little plant away, without asking any questions, began to grow. Little plant and her family noticed that the decision making capability of these humans had become very weak indeed and that thick heavy sleepiness had taken the place of clarity in their minds. They saw that the humans had mistaken the out-of-control feeling coming from ingesting the little plant for the human push towards the light. Thus, the humans had stopped hoping or praying, or even looking for a better way. This alarmed little plant and her family and, in a very short time, everything changed and peace was no more.

Little plant, growing peacefully and quietly on the land, is now surrounded by armed men, sometimes armed children too. Occasionally, during the endless push towards sunlight, a murdered human body falls down close by. Some of little plant's sisters have been killed by fallen bodies. Tiny children, with hands ripped to shreds, come and tend to little plant. She knows that these children are very sad and very scared. She sees desperation in the place of questioning, and sometimes she hears them talking to each other. One little girl's parents were murdered when she was very young by the same armed men that stomp about fearfully. She tried to run away but she was caught and beaten. She is very scared. Little plant tries to help by absorbing some of the little girl's fear.

One day, little plant gets harvested and is taken to a big barn where many people wearing masks and white coats are very busy. Little plant can see extreme fearfulness in every human's place of questioning. Little plant changes form into dried leaves. She is placed in a holding area. During this time, another group of armed men who look the same as the previous group, and present the same high levels of fearfulness raids the barn. The new group shoot and kill as many of the others as they can. Little plant sees scores of people murdered in one day. Little plant and her sisters are very distressed and have absorbed much fear from their experiences.

Little plant changes form again. She is now white and powdery and is placed inside hollow wooden ornaments and put into bags. A woman and her son drag the bags past uniformed men carrying large guns. The fear oozing from the pores of these two is too much for little plant, so she absorbs some of it in order to help the woman and her child.

The next few months are the most hectic in little plant's existence. She finds herself here and there, always moving, one day to the next, a new human in a new place. In each new setting she sees money change hands, less and less each time. With each new human owner, she becomes weaker and weaker as, oftentimes, they place a strange lifeless substance alongside her. One day she witnesses the violent stabbing of one of the men looking after her in order that she might be looked after by someone else. No money changed hands that day.

Little plant is tired of this journey; this world tour of murder, exploitation, fear, and greed. Finally, she reaches the end of her journey; a middle class, bespoke kitchen surface in Muswell Hill, North London. This is the end of the road for little plant. But she brings with her every drop of fear she has absorbed from her beginnings.

This is something of the truth of our recreational drug use; that which we manage to justify, especially as the rich and famous are doing it constantly and openly, even though it does happen to be illegal. Although this story is probably about cocaine or heroin, it also holds true for less destructive highs, such as cannabis. The corruption and devastation in the production of the illegal drugs we consume is forgotten in favour of the anticipation of a wild night ahead. This is also true of many other commodities we buy without question; evading awareness of the pain and suffering of millions that goes into bringing these useless items to us. However, of all trades, the drug trade is where the liar has the largest investment, as it is the trade which brings destruction and conflict to everyone it meets along the supply chain; from the very beginning, as a seed is planted, to the very end, when the narcotic-exacerbated liar might incite a bitter yuppie fallout. Each step along the way is laden with fear and carnage.

Convinced by the media and society that the drug trade is uninteresting, we look on cheerlessly as people we know and love crash and burn, sometimes fatally, due to getting hooked on drugs. Sometimes we hear stories of the reality of the trade, but we quickly forget. We'd rather not know; if the truth be told. The things that go on in the name of the drug trade are truly barbaric, but none of us cares. We are blind to our own complicity. Yet, if the drug trade reveals how interconnected we are, and therefore how responsible we are for great suffering in the world, it will have given us a useful perceptual gift.

We might be reasonably sane and see clearly that the trade is in hell, from start to finish. Or we may keep quiet when another person promotes drug use, for fear of losing face; there's an awful lot of that going on, subtly and not so. We may even promote drug use ourselves, having convinced ourselves of its coolness and better-than-ness, without looking too closely at what we are championing. Yet, no matter how hard we try, we cannot seem to do anything about the problem when it reaches proportions we can no longer deny. Perhaps our grown-up child is fighting addiction. Perhaps we are too, without accepting it. Perhaps all the youngsters in our societies are regularly high. Perhaps nearly everyone we know takes drugs and that, illogically, makes it OK.

Whether it is governments fighting cartels or parents praying their children will quit methamphetamine, the more we fight and war against it, the more impotent we are. The cartels hunker down, fuelled by continued demand. Our children disappear for longer and longer, fuelled by deeper feelings of worthlessness. The truth is that drugs supply a huge psychological need.

If anything proves the collective low self-esteem and profound unhappiness of the human race, it is our overwhelming need to hide behind addictions and distract ourselves continuously. Anything that can incapacitate our conscious processes to the degree that drugs do is our best option, because then we might escape from ourselves entirely. We hate ourselves so much, all of us, that anything that obscures this reality becomes a valued commodity. Once hooked into altered states of mind that provide - for short ecstatic moments - fools-happiness and false better-than-ness, we are truly lost.

Actually the drug trade is more than just appalling. We might rename it the slave-master trade; roll up, roll up for increased mental slavery and devastation, plus a hand in untold horrors the world over. Now, we even have a legitimate drug trade, whereby we might get high legally and pay drug companies instead of cartels. The market in oblivion is very lucrative indeed. The only real difference is in which side has been labelled good or bad, and these days it is difficult to tell the difference as the liar's activities become much more brazen and overt, seemingly impossible to challenge.

We are compelled to avoid reality by hiding behind something. Whether it is addiction to work, our boyfriend, food, stamp collecting, or crack cocaine, the liar in the mind need exert precious little effort in persuading us to keep treading the road to doom. The drug trade is simply the extreme end of this business, while puzzle writers and publishers are at the softer end of the same trade that supplies the human need to avoid becoming aware of the truth. When we are unhappy we use addictions to cover over our pain and, by doing so, we cushion our hearts from that which we cannot bear. When we are not so unhappy, we use addictions to avoid noticing our own babbling mind because, when we do notice it, what we find there makes us tremendously uncomfortable.

The addictive personality is one which has much to hide from itself. But the non-addictive personality, too, is living a dream; as far away from reality as the addict is. The *addictive personality* label is just another liar device, designed to convince us that some people are much worse than us, diverting attention from the fact that we are not at all different from each other, and neither are we having particularly different experiences of the world.

The drug trade, with all its depravity, is inevitable because the liar's beliefs form the foundation of our world. The belief in profit over all other considerations drives the cold exploitation of the underprivileged in poor countries. The lure of wealth, women, and *respect* in the mind of the wide-eyed, Western youngster, easily persuades him to get involved in the mayhem. The liar's ideas support it all, whichever way we look. The *war* on drugs is also part of the liar's game in that, if we are honest with ourselves, we may realise that we in the West are outraged that these worse-thans - people from poorer countries - could be getting extremely rich. This is simply not allowed; they might get wealthy enough to attack us successfully, so action must be taken quickly, before they do.

Not too far away from the insane justifications of senselessness, is the real devastation of the drug trade, in which small children are forced to work on pain of death, where land destined for food crops is poisoned, where the small children of farmers who refuse to plant opium are kidnapped and used as sex slaves. The West fares no better. No-one has a monopoly on the suffering arising from this business. Our kids get addicted to drugs, and the crime required to pay for them, perpetuating our insanely violent societies. It is only the wealthy - the tiniest, yet loudest, most visual and undoubtedly most better-than proportion of us - that seem to get away with drug use. However, only the wealthy have the resources to pay for the drugs and any fall out that might occur from their use. Nevertheless, whichever way you look, the drug trade wreaks devastation and breaks hearts.

When people stop getting high or drunk after years of substance or alcohol abuse, and start doing their personal healing work, they suddenly notice that they have not progressed emotionally from the very moment the addiction began. All development stopped right there. Getting high arrests personal growth and prevents us from maturing emotionally, no matter which drug they took or in what setting. This is the desired effect in any case, so we should not be surprised to hear it.

We are able to convince ourselves that everything we do is beneficial. Many people have managed to talk themselves into believing that certain drugs are useful when taken *recreationally*. The liar decrees we destroy ourselves, but it needs to make some justification for it, and so all the stories we hear about becoming enlightened by eating a mushroom or by drinking a vile concoction in the Andes are invented and exaggerated in order to lull us into a false sense of security.

Certain Indian holy men believe that by smoking a ton of pot they will become enlightened. They've been smoking pot for thousands of years now and I don't think one of them has succeeded yet. They have yet to figure out it doesn't work. This is just another form of the liar's promises that don't deliver; a very clear one too. Our innovation in dreaming up justifications for addiction is limitless; enlightenment might be the most ridiculous of them. The truth is that nothing comes from drugs; nothing at all, because if something beneficial did come from taking drugs, we might have stopped needing to take them the moment we did.

Forgiving the drug trade is, again, down to understanding it to be an inevitable part of the human world that does not know its own mind, nor wish to. Humans, under the liar's dictatorship, need to hide from their thoughts and any addictive tendency will do. Drugs, particularly the more potent ones, are the liar's offerings. *Take this and sleep*, it bids us. *You won't need to worry about your dreadful life anymore. Sleep-sleeep.* Or, even better: *Take this, now, and become so deranged you might do something wonderfully ruinous.* We follow the orders, convinced we are not making any mistake at the time, even though we always experience the resultant pain and regret.

Forgiving the farmers and the growers comes down to understanding that poverty can lead us into many dark corners, and we would be enticed into exactly the same activity if we were as poor and desperate. We forgive the rich growers, using violence and fear to exploit the locals, by understanding that the mind of the grower is stuck on *profit over all other considerations*, just like the rest of us. Again, if we were in the same position, we would be just as demented.

Forgiving the traffickers, pushers, and dealers on the street is the same empathic leap into the shoes of those souls who have become so insane they have managed to justify the unthinkable and, from doing so, built worlds in which the unthinkable is the daily norm. Yet what else could they have done given their circumstances and the lies they hold to be true? If we believe the liar to an intense degree, believing our status and value is dependent on how wealthy we are, how many women we own, and how violent we can be towards our human brothers, then the drug trade is an ideal occupation.

We forgive those of us who decide to use drugs to go deeper into unawareness, and we forgive those of us who have become so distressed that drugs seemed to be the only answer to our unceasing cry for love and compassion. We forgive the war on drugs because it is irrational, illogical, and governed entirely by the liar in the human mind.

We condone none of this either, instead seeing the pain and suffering that our brothers are going through. In place of the *evil* and condemned, we see tormented minds. We know that our world could not be any other way given our state of mind, our deep fearfulness, our belief in guilt, and our inability to see anything clearly. The drug trade is a symptom of our shared psychosis.

The liar tells us to drink this, take this, and promises we will experience heaven. We believe the liar and obey it repeatedly. We never notice its continued broken promise, even though we only ever reach hell. This is why we must call this thing the liar. When we see how we have been tricked so mercilessly and for so long, we must surely wake up.

We believe that hell is heaven, and so we chase eternally after destruction. This is why *treats* always hurt us. We call them sinful, chuckling as if that were a good thing and didn't matter. Some of us might consider drugs entirely commonplace, but we all know the truth deep down. Perhaps our privileged status has us in an environment in which getting high is reasonable and desirable. Except that, yet again, without trying, the liar reveals itself in that the better-than state of the rich and privileged reeks of the deepest, dirtiest, most difficult prison to escape from; the eye of the needle indeed.

In truth, sober in the present moment is the new high. I wonder what the world will look like when we all agree on that. From the sober present moment we might heal our minds, discard all useless and self-destructive beliefs, and watch while a new peaceful world forms itself around the choices we make based on peace and love alone.

Forgiving all the characters and role players in the drug trade means we must ultimately forgive ourselves for the total mess we have made with the misused creative potential of our conscious minds and the beautiful abundant paradise that we share. No doubt, we will have preferred some altered state to hanging out with the Big G. We will have to forgive ourselves this too. Yes, the present moment with a clear and sober mind is Heaven.com and, no matter what great insights we think we have gleaned from altered states of consciousness, life without the liar is leading us here.

15 MONSANTO

Our world is out of control. We don't have to look too hard to see it. If we don't end up annihilating everything in an all-out super-war, we might instead weaken our immune systems with endless unnecessary medications and toxic food to the extent that we are wiped out completely by a super-bug. Perhaps our tampering with the delicate ecosystems of the world will cause environmental disasters from which few of us emerge unscathed, or maybe we will end up dying of starvation for the same reason.

Does all this sound like a price worth paying for temporary, material, and essentially meaningless riches? Of course not; but this is where we stand. Our current situation puts us as close to the liar's end goal as we have ever been, and we are all doing our bit; by our weekly shop, or filling the car, or believing anything that anyone in a white coat says, or insisting our children's problems at school are due to brain chemistry imbalances, or supporting conflict and war in regions of the world we cannot even pronounce. The liar has never had it so good. Be clear; every one of the cataclysms that seems to be just about to happen is the liar's intention and we are its zombie workforce.

In a single, isolated physical body - which we have been told, and believed, is the sole ruler of the universe and thus due unlimited importance - the liar's business is mainly restricted to personal relationship disharmony. In groups and organisations, the liar has more power at its disposable and the effects of believing it can be devastating. But if the single body was indeed the sole ruler of the universe - as we are told repeatedly - why should the liar need to form collective liar-minds that may act as a single entity in order to accomplish even more damage? This suggests that the liar itself does not accept its own tenet on separation. The fact is that, the liar is so insane, it may circumvent even its own beliefs in order to pursue its deranged objective.

Currently, Monsanto is the bad boy of the group formations we have built to do the liar's dirty work at a larger scale. However, Monsanto is far from alone in its devilry, and even the most innocuous of companies will be compulsively adding to our problems; as will each and every one of us, whether we like it or not. This ball of confusion and fear got rolling a long, long time ago. We simply did not notice it picking up speed in the last few hundred years and, with momentum gaining, pulling all and sundry along with it.

Monsanto is the current flag-flyer for all corporations that seem hell bent on the destruction of the natural world. Every time I look at my Facebook news feed, I see someone moaning about Monsanto, about how *evil* they are, and how they must be stopped immediately. Agreed; if anyone is doing anything that might destroy our home, they should be stopped; at least, we should do what we can; it is our obligation as caretakers of the earth and the only sane response to the environmental lunacy we are seeing today. However, the idea that Monsanto, and those that work for it, are *evil* is nonsense.

We are sure that all those working for Monsanto, and similar organisations, are evil, arrogant and wicked; condemnable human beings. We point the finger, curse them, and wish them dead. But wait, hang on a minute, doesn't your great aunt Doreen work in a Monsanto factory; surely she's not evil? Oh, no, actually no, not Doreen. Doreen is one of the poor exploited ones, oppressed by the evil managers. It's the managers that are evil. Yes, the managers are the devil incarnate. But, wait a minute; my brother-in-law's cousin is a manager at Monsanto. You know, Dave. He's a great guy, a loving family man. Ahem, no, not the managers actually, sorry, um, it's the shareholders, they're the evil ones. Yes, let's kill all the shareholders. Um, but hang on a minute, I have shares in Monsanto, I received them years ago as part of a legacy. Ahem, well, OK. Um, no. Um, it's the owner, yes. He must be the evil one. Yes. That's it! The owner of Monsanto is the evil one, Satan himself. Um, actually, don't the shareholders own Monsanto?

It's not too difficult to see how becoming indignant and irate can only be the liar's influence again. It loves getting us riled up, persuading us to point the finger at phantoms, and wish slow, lingering deaths on Monsanto workers, managers, and shareholders, as if they were nothing like us and as if that might solve the underlying problem. The liar is a master evader.

Actually, the *corporation* is probably as close as we have gotten to *evil* in many senses. To explain this we must look at the perceptual process of projection which, as we have seen, is automatic and constant. We project our guilt away from ourselves in order that we might be free of it. That this process is ineffective, and we never find ourselves free of guilt, makes no difference, we keep trying. Guilt may take innumerable forms and the liar insists that by projecting it we will save ourselves. We find - or invent - a target for our guilt and start accusing, becoming irate with and aggressive towards our chosen blame-holder. We point the finger and condemn and, by doing so, we manage to justify the inexcusable; while the liar rubs its hands, mission complete. And whatever we think we see externally when we are angry, is exactly what we will find within our own minds when we look closely enough.

Ironically, this projecting business of this liar who insists on the reality of our separateness and isolation is only viable in a mind that is aware of our true connection. So it is no surprise to see that this projecting business is not limited to guilt. Indeed, anything at all that we are thinking and feeling becomes painted onto the external space around us. Artists reveal their innermost feelings and beliefs through their work. The media reveals the sick human mind in its pathological state. The love that we truly are is also constantly projecting itself, everywhere, but we see it very little, unsurprisingly. It is therefore logical that we might project even the liar itself onto our external canvas.

The liar is a cold, ruthless, conflict-inciting machine with no remorse. It believes it is the sole ruler of the universe and fights tooth and nail to defend this unattainable position. It believes that, as king of all, it should own everything; material things, people, the mind space, and knowledge. It believes that profiting in any of these, over all other considerations, is a natural law of the universe. It believes that fear is real and brutally ensures that this belief is never contested. How might we have projected such a mad concept into the world?

Under the liar's mind control, we have edged ever closer to building its representation here on earth. In the past, we invented the devil and that sufficed as the liar's representative, but we don't believe in such nonsense anymore, not really. Instead, nowadays we have tangible, examinable, and functioning representations of the liar in the world - corporations, which we have accepted as normal; as if we would have happily invited Satan to our homes for tea and a chat a few hundred years ago.

Corporations are autonomous - supporting the liar's belief in separateness. They have been constructed in such a way that they cannot be held accountable for their activities or motivations - supporting the liar's despotic reign over everything. The single aim of a corporation is profit over all other considerations, the liar's incessant mantra to our beleaguered ears. This is our world and we champion it endlessly, without realising the lunacy in doing so. It can be a scary moment seeing just where our collective insanity has led us; the production of god-like *bodies* that have every power at their disposal for maintaining, reconfirming, and extending the belief in the separateness, inequality, and meaninglessness of all life. Corporations are the human race's Frankenstein monster.

Corporations may well be the most dastardly projection coming from the liar in our minds, and the closest in content to its fuller self; that which, if we were able to witness it in its entirety, would terrify us beyond belief. Worst still, these corporations have an inbuilt function; the ability to destroy their own maker. Like cancer, they murder the hand that feeds them. I give a fuller description of why corporations can only be the liar's invention in my first book which describes the liar's functionality in greater detail.

I was going to list a few of the unhelpful practices of Monsanto here, but you can look them up yourselves, they're no secret. In any event, Monsanto is likely not the worst of corporations - in terms of how destructive they have been towards life on our planet - so cataloguing their outrageous actions serves no real purpose. What is notable - and again not limited to Monsanto - is their chosen practice of protecting their mistakes by not admitting them when they should, just like we all have done at one time. The silence of companies when something goes badly wrong is due to the incessant liar mantra of *profit over all other considerations*; as it is with us, personally, too. Corporations notoriously protect profits at the expense of everyone, including every single person that works for them.

But what do they do? Monsanto develops biotechnology and produces chemicals which support enhanced product growth. They offer more profit to farmers and industry, and are in it to get rich. That is it. Any of the *bad* things that they have done - and they have been very naughty, on more than one occasion - is due to the fear of being poor. Simple. And you and I act exactly the same way due to the same fear, albeit at a level that has no obvious effect on the global environment. But I do, and so do you. So we should stop complaining about what we do ourselves, just because it happens to take a more intense form. In truth, it is the same. When a pebble is dropped into the pond, we don't know where each ripple might end up, but the pebble is the only cause of the ripples. I'm on one ripple, you're on another, and Monsanto is sat on the corporation ripple that is threatening to become a giant tsunami, ready to engulf everything.

If we ignore our own complicity, point the finger, and become indignant, righteous, and angry, we are still the liar's zombie and just being led evasively around the issue. In addition, any solution we might cook up to solve the problem of the runaway corporation train must arise, logically, from the same set of values that caused the problem in the first place, the liar-mind. Perhaps we might see angry activist-types setting up new forms of organisational governance in the future, and perhaps there will be a short period of *getting it nearly right*; but if no-one has resolved the liar in the human mind - our species-wide perceptual pathology - it will not be too long before the situation becomes critical again. The liar's solutions are always more of the same.

Success, as the liar has it - and who else does have it right now? - is based on manipulation of the worse-thans; that which we consider reasonable, all of us. The bullying in the school playground is simply our children imitating what they have seen in everyone's mind. Our disdain for those we hold a grudge against or who we consider evil means we don't care that they are hurting. We exploit the poorer parts of the world by rampant looting of natural resources, with no concern for anything at all, and if anyone does end up suffering or dying because of our actions, they were non-human anyway, worse-than, as worth saving as a fly in the kitchen. As long as our personal needs are met, we don't care about anything. This is an undeniable symptom of the separation psychosis from which we all suffer.

Monsanto is just an extreme example of how we all *take advantage* of the apparently vulnerable. Because it is a giant corporation, it is able to use its power to take as much advantage as it can and this, obviously, has massive effects in the world. All of us take advantage, however. Few of us just like to be; to simply be with others, enjoying communication. More often than not, there is an ulterior motive to our relationships. We might not speak to each other at all unless we want something for ourselves.

Why is it so difficult to see that what is in our own minds is a mirror image of the activities of the external world? The liar will tell us otherwise; but when we cease to value the false beliefs and ideas we have cherished for eons, we will start to see. The outside world is only violent and terrifying when we feel the same fear about ourselves and each other. It becomes easier when we realise the glistening truth that none of us are in any way perceptually different from anyone else. Perhaps that's a terrifying idea. As long as it is, we're doomed.

Is Monsanto the world's most evil corporation? a headline reads. No, Monsanto is just one of the more successful *bodies* we have set up for doing the liar's bidding. Monsanto is probably not the most successful corporation playing the liar's game - success here defined in terms of wanton destruction of life - but it has certainly become the most well-known for its unhelpfulness. Maybe we can use this as a clear example for explaining the diseased mind of humanity to humans yet to see it. Then, one day, we might be able to be grateful that its outrages pushed us towards truth. But, in the meantime, like the problem alcoholic, we will point at the world around us, complaining bitterly about it, yet refusing to become aware of our obvious complicity in the mess of our life which has been, in fact, caused by us alone.

Profit is the god of humanity, assigning dark representatives to govern its minions in the external world. Those that work for these current-day demons are hooked into the corporate way of thinking, just like wobbly-eyed, religious cult members, managing to excuse and overlook the most unhelpful of activities. These workers have talked themselves into believing that the corporation they belong to (work for) and its ways are their personal path to salvation. How easily we lose sense and autonomy when better-than status and personal profit is promised if we speak the lies and follow the orders we believe to be unquestionable. We rarely notice how deeply unhappy we are playing this game and never winning.

We are judged and appraised by fellow members of the corporate cult - those who are a little better than us - on how much profit we have managed to grab for our god. We talk in cyphers and newspeak, covering up the truth of our destructive activities. We feel far better than those in the starving villages we have just left without clean water for months by clicking a button on our screen, and we are rewarded for that click which earned the company millions. We are loathed by many of our co-workers, and all our underlings, and those we consider friendly would turn on us in an instant, as we would them. Open conflict has become wholly acceptable in the corporate world and we are ready to stand up and vouch for this lunacy; that which is more excessive than the carryings on in any serious psychotic ward at the asylum. This lunacy is our daily bread.

Today, the liar is so out of control, it has found itself in the amazing position of being able to be completely honest with us. It does not have to hide itself, or be evasive, in the corporate world. The blatant honesty of the corporate world is jaw-dropping at times. Sometimes when I hear the things that people say - in all seriousness and without fear of inciting a bad opinion - I can hardly believe my ears.

Recently, I found myself among a group of people who were deeply committed to their jobs, their god-like employers, and their corporate lifestyles. The conversations were a continued cataloguing of all the reasons why each person must be better than the others. The things that apparently elevated the better-than status were which school you had gone to, where you lived - and for sure it could not be Chicago or any suburb, anywhere - who you knew and, of course, which corporation had taken over your mind and whereabouts on the corporate ladder you found yourself. The chat was boring and predictable. At some point these men and women, showing off to each other, seemed to morph into a group of male apes puffing up their chests, growling and hissing menacingly, bearing their teeth and posing in competition.

One of the top dogs was telling us about the recent industrial activities of the Chinese. She detailed their amassing of natural resources from Africa and how they were being rather naughty in business. She told us what these African countries were losing in terms of raw materials and revenue, how badly they were faring from the deals, and how many billions the Chinese we making from the deals. She painted a bleak picture, with the liar all over it, of course. She then mentioned that it was just like the European colonialism of old; the fortunes that could be made were astronomical. *So, why wouldn't you?* she said, in all seriousness.

Anyone with a modicum of sanity can see clearly the million reasons as to why we wouldn't behave like this - profiting over all other considerations - but currently most of us don't have that capacity and, indeed, yes, we too would take advantage over the less-thans in order to profit. We make and agree with remarks just like this all the time, without seeing the madness therein. This is the liar; a thought construct so tenacious, so precise, so efficient, it has us completely under its control and we have no idea it is there. The liar is well ahead of the game and I know that well enough to avoid confronting it head on. The liar senses any attack on its foundations immediately and, in a mind locked into doing its bidding, becomes irate and aggressive when challenged, and liable to goodness knows what level of conflict. This is the corporate world.

Just like you and I might fight bitterly over a pay rise, even though neither of us is struggling to survive in any real sense, corporations will fight, tooth and nail, over a resource, land, or how they appear on TV, regardless of who and what they must destroy. The process is never ending; we are all chasing the same old and tired liar's promise, yet again. *If you get this thing, you will be happy*, it says. And we get this thing, whatever it is, but we are not happy. Profit cannot satisfy, by the liar's design because, if it did, we'd stop chasing it. Profit is just another substitute for that which we believe is missing from our lives and makes them seem empty and meaningless.

The illegal drug trade we just mentioned is barely distinct from the corporate world. The only obvious difference these days is the legality which, for the drug trade, means it is not tied into hiding and covering up its messy, nefarious activities. The legitimate corporate world gets closer and closer to being as honest as it likes about its criminal conduct too. There seems nothing that it will not do, no-one it will not step on to get its way. There is also no government which is not deeply entwined in the business of the corporate world, whether they wish to be or not. At this level, even legality is usurped by better-than, worse-than, and profit over all other considerations.

The liar invented Monsanto and its cohorts, and we didn't. The peaceful and content human beings that we truly are, underneath the madness, could not have dreamt up such a nightmare. Utilising its corporate army most efficiently, the liar is now gleefully destroying our abundant paradise, right under our noses. While it does so, we either join in, flying the flag of profit over all other considerations as if it were a divine edict, or point the finger viciously at the *evil* ones, not realising we should be pointing the same finger at ourselves first.

We built these devastation machines, fired them up, and they got going. The problem is that, now, we cannot stop them. Monsanto is the focus of our indignation about unjust business practices and the mess we are making in the natural world, but all corporations function similarly, to profit over all other considerations with no responsibility to life on earth. Even green corporations and charities can only do so much because they will be set up in exactly the same way; organisationally overseen by the liar and peopled by humans suffering from the same psychosis, that which is intent on destruction.

We delight in moaning about corporations, but we are all the same as they are. The only real difference is in the number of people - aside from ourselves - we may affect detrimentally by our actions. When we take advantage of our friend's naïve kindness at school, we hurt each other. When we utter megalomaniacal statements at work for fear of what people might think, or losing our jobs, or because we've become exceptionally insane, we hurt ourselves and our human family. When we profit from the inability of a nation to stop us from plundering their natural resources, we hurt ourselves and millions of others. But each of these acts is exactly the same in content.

The corporate world is just another logical, inevitable, and expected result of the mental problem we all share in equal measure; a symptom of the cause and not the cause itself. When we see that what is outside is simply a reflection of what is going on inside everyone's perception, with no exceptions, we can no longer condemn or point the finger; it just doesn't make any sense to do so. Assuming that somehow Monsanto and its ilk are *evil* and different to us is a mistaken interpretation of reality, dished up to us by the liar. And how could it be any other way?

However, did Monsanto force us to accidentally stumble upon yet another marvellous component of our new forgiveness model? In forgiving Monsanto properly, and all the corporations that seem to be dead set on destroying the world in their pursuit of profit, we are forced to forgive ourselves at the same time. As without, so within. Moreover, this is true of all the unforgivables we have examined, and will ever examine. We forgive ourselves by understanding that all our troubles come from a species-wide insanity that no-one has avoided. We forgive ourselves because we finally see that our own actions are the same in content as those of the corporations we detest. We forgive ourselves because we know there can be nothing that humans do not share. This new forgiveness holds within it the power to change the world. And it looks like nothing else will be able to do so, permanently.

16 FUKUSHIMA

It seems pertinent to add a short chapter on the Fukushima nuclear disaster as, perceptually, this is an excellent example of where the liar-mind will lead us while we know nothing about it.

When profit over all other considerations is our god, anything that obstructs our fervent worship will, at first, be ignored. In the case of nuclear reactors, we ignore the fact that they are decrepit and should be taken out of service for safety reasons. Instead, we would rather keep these megaliths running, bringing in the bucks, even though they are worryingly old and leaky.

When an obstacle to profit cannot be ignored for whatever reason, we may then ridicule it. In the case of nuclear energy, the voices against it have always been tarnished as barmy, hippy, counter-culture types, not worthy of consideration; but perhaps we do not believe this so much these days.

When ridicule becomes ineffective, we might attack the obstacle to our worship, and violent criminality is not off the menu here. Even a tangible, on-going, and undeniable threat to the lives and well-being of those that profit from rickety nuclear power stations is no obstacle to the madness continuing.

While we label the destruction of man-made, temporary, and meaningless things criminal vandalism, we consider the destruction of the natural world as legal progress. Again, these are human beliefs not limited to some *evil* ones over there. We all share the liar's world view. When we follow our bizarre and senseless convictions to their bitter - yet logical - end results, we are bound to build systems and machines that can destroy us outright. We obviously forgot that we too are part of the natural world.

When we cannot stop these life-destroying machines, organisations, and systems, we must have reached the pinnacle of our insanity and as close to the liar's end goal as we have ever been. We are sure that those locked up inside mental institutions are the insane ones; but in fact, those poor souls simply cannot cope with the madness going on outside.

When a corporate entity or governmental organisation - and all the madness entailed therein - controls power and energy, and has at its disposal a particularly dangerous element that may destroy the earth and every living thing that resides on it, oh, the liar cannot contain its excitement and anticipation. Couple that with an inability to take into account public safety - something we somehow forget must always include ourselves - due to the overarching goal of *lining our pockets* and we have a ticking time-bomb. Well, we all knew that, didn't we? I'm not telling anyone anything they didn't know already.

Human safety is simply not an issue when it comes to making money. When we overlook cheaper and safer forms of energy production in preference to what we know to have an inherent and serious danger potential for all life on earth, we surely must admit our insanity. And now, nearly three years after the tsunami in 2011 that killed 20,000 and brought the nuclear plant at Fukushima to its knees, the ruined reactor continues to spew deadly radioactive waste into the environment at an alarming rate. The clean-up operation is a massive fail. We can only wait and see what might happen now. But it was only a matter of time, wasn't it?

It is impossible to cover this one up with rhetoric and platitudes, so we rarely hear about it in the media, which prefers to fill our heads with less important things, maintaining the daily, constant hypnotic suggestion that the world as we have it is normal and OK; that the aggressive, violent, competitive winner is OK; that the mutilated woman is OK.

Did you know that most of the nuclear plants in operation right now should have been shut down years ago? They have a life span which we have blatantly ignored in order to keep them running way past their sell-by dates. Cheap, clean, and renewable energy has been available for donkey's years, maybe centuries. But we must serve our god and get rich, so we overlook it, or silence it, or do whatever we can to maintain our personal profit and remain the winner; except, by the liar's design, the winners will always be the eventual losers. Perhaps we can go to Mars and start the destruction all over again. It is just a matter of time.

Profit is god, profit is king, and profit drives us, whether we are a corporate entity, a small business, a sole trader or just a regular person on the street. We become blind to common sense in the pursuit of profit or the desperate actions we are prepared to take in order to protect what we have already amassed. Yet we are so angered by those shadowy evil ones, playing with our lives and our children's futures, just

142

to get rich. *How dare they?* we bark, hypocritically.

Well, Fukushima did end up scaring the bejesus out of everyone at the time and some out-of-date nuclear reactors were quickly shut down. Now we have *fracking* as a replacement money-making energy source which has its own share of horrible environmental payoffs. No, we can't even learn our lesson the hard way. We simply replace one perilous, energy production process with another.

Just like the Large Hadron Collider, which may or may not be able to destroy the world...braking hard...what!? May or may not? Doesn't the tiniest doubt like that insist we take the possibility seriously? Even if the doubt is miniscule, the world, our home, is surely not something we'd be happy risking? Would it? Sadly, yes, it seems. The desperate race to explain all life as a process of matter - the liar's game for sure - is much more important than the continuance of the world itself. God, we're so insane.

The world is a total mess and it is all down to the insanity of the human race which can be easily explained by the liar-mind model of perception I'm putting forward. Solutions to any of our problems will not be found within the same system of perception; that which ensures the continued occurrence of disasters like Fukushima. When we play by the rules of the system, we have assumed there is nothing wrong with the system and so there is nothing there to fix or escape from. The system itself does not know it is pathological, just like the intensely insane are not aware they are insane. The liar has won. And the liar will continue to win as long as we are allied with it.

There is no-one to point the finger at either, unless we are pointing it at ourselves as well as our chosen bad guys. We split the atom then used the science to destroy our enemies. Now we use it to profit at the expense of safety. We are the bad guys. All those who said anything against our insanity were labelled worse-than, hippies, and the money machine rolled on in relative peace. But it was only a matter of time, right?

Those who should speak up when they see danger looming, or an immediate peril, or an emergency the world needs to know about, rarely say anything because of the fear of what others might think. In some cases, we are too fearful of our personal safety to be strong-minded enough to blow the whistle on madness that may detrimentally affect millions. We have noticed that the brave souls who do speak up usually end up in prison for decades, at best. More commonly, the liar has our minds in such a vice-like grip, we dare not offend the others, or look bad, or lose face, and so we never go against the grain, against the party line. Our arrogance knows no bounds as we preserve our illusory better-than status at the cost of all life on the planet, literally.

I wonder if those who witnessed the liar in the human mind in the remote past could have had any idea how bad things could be when enough organised, liar-driven humans were around to supply its demands at large-scale intensity? They must have seen the ingenuity in its ability to constantly evade discovery by refocusing the mind on something else, and then another thing, always skirting around the point that might unmask it. The liar is not a new idea and I certainly didn't make it up. It is difficult to see though. Those that did, many thousands of years ago, wrote about what they saw. But the problem is so deeply engrained that those descriptions have been easily obfuscated by misunderstanding and reinterpretation.

In the Hollywood blockbusters, the baddie is often the corrupt official, e.g. the local mayor who doesn't give a hoot that a shark is eating the people in his town, because profit is far more important than other people's lives. This is a marvellous Hollywood archetype that is seen in many films. The good guys always arrive on time to clean up the mess of such fools and zombies. Sadly, we are lacking a good guy to clean up the mess of the insane supporters of nuclear fuel and fracking, as well as the global-warming deniers and the like. Or if there is a good guy - and I know there is - he will not be operating from within the liar's system of thought, so his appearance may be unexpected and surprising. He may also be missed for the same reason.

There is a better way; we simply cannot see it with all the muck in our eyes. There is always a solution to any problem because the truth, outside of the liar's thought-system, is that the universe is benevolent, loving, and kind, and very much wants us to be happy. However, we have placed an obstacle between the loving kindness of the universe and our own true selves. This is the liar. Get rid of it, problem solved. Keep it, keep the problem. The liar is the only problem we have.

17 THE NAZIS

The liar operates in a single person's thought processes, causing havoc and upset within relationships and life experiences. That the thoughts and beliefs inciting our private pain are no different from the next person's is rarely seen and, instead, we believe our personal experience of life to be entirely unique, shared by no-one, and usually needing to be kept as secret as possible. The grudge we hold against our colleague at work we consider justified, as well as original. The fact is that everyone else in the office is holding similarly formed grudges against other colleagues. The hateful mantras we utter to ourselves, justifying the condemnation, are practically the same, and someone else hates us just as much. There is no separateness, in truth. And even our apparently diverse and individual physical appearances would confuse an alien from another planet. They all look the same! he would likely declare.

When one person's belief is shared by another and not kept hidden, the liar forms a group belief system that, ironically and unintentionally, proves we must be interconnected. When we share a belief, it gains power, even when it is not true. Shared beliefs become rooted and immutable, locked into the thought processes of group members, and dished out to new arrivals to the group, whether they request them or not. Ideas held by the group are rarely challenged; this is what is happening inside corporations and other organisational bodies. In the same way a single person may defend his personal space, relationships, owned objects, and the ideas he may hold to be true - bitterly and violently at times - so too does the group. The underlying content of any formation based on shared ideas, in the liar's world, is always equivalent; attack first before the inevitable attack comes from outside.

There will still be disharmony within larger groups at the personal level, and in subgroup infighting, but the group themes remain untouchable throughout the collective, becoming powerfully soporific. If a member dares question the key tenets of the group, they forfeit membership, at best. At birth, we automatically become members of groups like this, the labels of which include gender, relative wealth, social status, language, and culture, for example. We do not seem to have a choice about membership of these groups and, for this reason, find it hard to break free of them.

A culture's group experience mirrors the personal life experience in that whatever happened to it in the past forms its beliefs, characteristics, and predispositions. This is particularly true when there has been big upheaval in the group's history, inciting certain unquestionable beliefs to form which promote common and idiosyncratic reactions to situations. If a cultural group has experienced high levels of suffering at the hands of others in the past, a worse-than theme may become apparent in the group psyche. A single human being, who has been hurt very profoundly, prior to healing, will reveal such worse-than beliefs too. What is true for the person is true for the collective.

Desperate to offset worse-than, we are more easily seduced by the liar's insistence that we are better-than; the only deserving ones, the sole rulers of the universe. When the liar is seen for what it is, we may guffaw at the madness of these ideas - especially considering we are all hearing the same thing - but, in the meantime, when the worse-than becomes excruciating, we will grab at anything promising balm for our perceptual wounds. Becoming convinced of our better-than-ness serves just that purpose. This can get extremely exaggerated at times.

The liar's superior and better-than assurances are a cover-up for slightly less dishonest beliefs in worse-than and inferiority. Whenever we look closely enough, we can see that the more intense the declaration of superiority, the more intense is the worse-than belief supporting it. Cultural worse-than beliefs come from the fallout from horrific experiences. The post-traumatic stress takes hold, cementing deeply fearful self-identities while it gains momentum and avalanches. At the same time and intensity, the group forms superiority complexes with the same intensity that suppress the poor-me perceptions coming from historical events. Furthermore, as we have seen time and time again, if something is truly superior, better-than, it would not need to keep on defending this state by using the liar's only defence strategy; destroying that which it has singled out as worse-than.

Great hurt causes psychotic reactions at varying degrees. No-one suffering from an obsessive compulsive disorder, ADHD, or any other labelled psychosis, has not suffered great hurt. The intensity of the perceptual fallout from whatever it was that caused such pain can be so intense, that OCD and similar become a way of smothering and silencing the wailing mind. There are unlimited examples of how we distract ourselves from our pain. I mention OCD because the German people are so well-known for their orderliness, efficiency, and organisational skills. This is not a bad thing at all. All cultural groups have their quirks and stereotypes but, like anything in the liar's world, these characteristics are not representative of what we truly are and are often distractions. Moreover, in some cases, these cultural idiosyncrasies can become exaggerated, unhelpful tools used by the liar in the mind for its dark purposes.

Our cultural predispositions can be expressed subtly or vigorously. When a group suffers great hardship, it is reasonable to assume such characteristics may become pronounced. If the group psyche is deep inside the liar's clutches, licking its wounds, it is also reasonable to assume that the liar will use such vulnerability for its own ends. When ideas take hold within a group, the predisposition of the group must play a part in the form they take externally; their presentation in words and actions. Sadly, although every instance of genocide is fundamentally the same in content, coming from the same lies that we all believe, no one group has ever managed to be as efficient at it as the Germans in World War II. The German approach to the extinction of millions was as if they were running a profitable business, not killing human beings.

How far will the liar in the human mind take us? There is no limit to the murderous capability of a person in the grips of the liar outside of opportunity and ability. The same can be said of the group's deadly intentions. Some of the most despotic regimes have often been rather haphazard and sporadic about the slaughtering. Genocide is usually sparked off by anger and rage in the killers. We might envision chaotic marauders, bellowing and growling while they decimate anything that moves. Strangely perhaps, the German slaughter of the Jewish people, and others they considered unfit to exist, revealed no obvious external rage or chaos. Instead, these emotions were internalised and calculating, causing organised, efficient, and wholly justified, state-sponsored murder.

Everything within is projected without. A belief in better-ness, so fixed and unshakeable, could well produce the levels of arrogance required for approaching the annihilation of millions like a project management exercise. This is our biggest warning yet. There is no way we could conceive of madness like this outside of complete liar-mind control. Adolf Hitler was clearly very insane and yet somehow he managed to persuade a whole nation to agree with his psychotic idealism. If they didn't agree, they kept very quiet about their dissent while, first, the physically and mentally disabled townsfolk disappeared, and then their Jewish neighbours.

The Nazi belief in better-than-ness was as far as it has got for the liar in the human mind. More importantly, this is as far as we may all go, given the right circumstances, opportunity, and an unshakeable false belief in our own superiority. The liar had those that labelled themselves *Nazi* believing they were the sole rulers of the universe, the singular *master race*, to the extent that they had to justify the inevitable and unthinkable. Anything that wasn't up to their bizarre *high* standards had no right to exist. We all share this idea at some level - the idea we are the sole rulers of the universe - but we rarely have the opportunity to express it to this intensity. However, this *unforgivable* is an example of how far our insanity may take us all.

The figure-head is always representative of the whole group and the ideas he expounds are shared by all members. We believe we could never idolise a lunatic in the same way the German people did, quietly forgetting that we adore Osho - regardless of his biochemical terrorist activities and emotional insecurity on relationships. Any shadowy guru figure that appeals to a preferred distraction of ours will do. We might reason with ourselves, illogically, that Osho can be excused because he did not poison 500 odd people with his own hands, but this is like saying that Hitler can be excused because he didn't turn the gas on himself.

Fear is an energy that permeates to the farthest reaches of the group-mind and we all suffer from it, in various forms, while we are here. The teachings of Hitler proved to the German people that they were better than others; that they were the superior race. Who, not knowing of the equality of all life, would not be seduced by such ranting? The teachings of criminal gurus may deliver the lie in a different form; but the group's perception soaks up and regurgitates any underlying fears which may cause the justification - at the highest level - of murder, sexual abuse, and other crimes. A sensitive person will always notice the disharmony inside groups where fear has been dressed up as love. We sense imbalance immediately on meeting a member of a fear-based group because attempting to communicate with such incongruous thought processes feels like walking into a solid object in the dark.

Yet, we are all the same and we all accept fear and pain as salvation every day, at varying levels of intensity. If we believe we wouldn't have been persuaded by Hitler, as the German people were, we must think there is something wrong with the Germans that we don't share.

Perhaps then we can label them worse-than and justify atrocities against them? And so the wheel of lies and devastation rolls on, just as the liar requires it. The liar became unusually organised in Nazi Germany. It got as close as it has ever been to building the empty, pathetic, and meaningless world it has in store for all its obedient winners; the only thing it can offer.

The systematic and abhorrent extermination techniques the Nazis employed in their attempts to exterminate the Jews were possible because they believed that the men, women, children, and babies they were murdering were non-human. They had convinced themselves of their superiority to the degree that they were able to dream up the notion of a world in which all those they didn't like weren't around. We all do this on a smaller scale every day; believing our playmate should die, our colleague should get the sack, the guy that just cut us up on the motorway should crash his car, or the dissenting population should be disappeared; and only then will we feel better. When this insane idea was put into form by the Nazis, the liar wreaked the most havoc it ever has, so far. We can also see the liar's game at its clearest - as long as we remain aware that we are all capable of the same thing.

That one human could be of less or more value than another is obviously not true. Even when we become deranged enough to believe and act on this false idea, we do not lose our connection to the truth of the matter, although it is usually buried deeply beneath the lunacy. A clinically insane person might believe the sun is an orange, but that belief would not stop the sun affecting him. As we have seen in the Atlantic slave trade, the fact that the Africans could not have been worse than the white Europeans meant a great effort was required to prove their worse-than-ness. So too did the Nazis need to prove the worse-than-ness of those earmarked for extinction. The justification process became rather like the extinction machine itself; cold, calculated, precise, and utterly insane.

The Nazis were heavily involved in academic pursuits, with scientists and doctors producing papers and giving talks at conferences as seemingly respectable as those of global academia today. Areas of study included *scientific* proofs of the less-than human state of non-healthy-bodied-Aryans, just like the studies on the black African a century or so before. Their scientific activities were excessive proofs of our mad belief in the supremacy of the body; as if the capacity to think were defined by the body's appearance alone, against the preponderance of proof to the contrary. Not only that, but the non-humans singled out by the Nazis and discarded in the camps were used as lab rats for grotesque *scientific* experimentation. Logically, a human being re-identified as non-human has the same rights as an animal, perhaps less.

One of the few things that non-human life doesn't do when compared with humans, is to seek for God or meaning. This does not mean that if a human being decides he has found God or meaning he has necessarily found anything of value. And just because our Western culture now has a predominantly secular tone, does not mean we are not still searching for a representation of God or meaning in our lives. In fact, the hunt for meaning, for purpose, is something we all undoubtedly share. The Nazis operated under atheist and scientific principles; effectively a not-God religion. But just because there isn't a god to worship does not mean something else must take its place.

The human psyche, under the liar's dictatorship, has built something like a pantheistic religion, in which a number of worldly things operate as representations of the overall divinity; which is the liar itself, of course. We worship those ideas and forms which most closely relate to the liar's worldview. We have already noted that one of our gods is *profit* and there can be little disagreement with that. The body, of course, is another. Yet another, relatively modern projection of the liar's model of perception is science, that which depends upon the belief in separation as truth, i.e. objectivity. The god of science is that secular ideology which apparently established Nazism, in the words of Hitler himself. Interestingly enough, science is usually a pretty heartless, calculated, and detached affair. Indeed, in many ways those are its prerequisites.

The meaning and purpose we are desperate to find is nowadays expected to be delivered by science. The liar's game is totally logical and profoundly insane. Science as god assists the liar splendidly. It has us distracted with deconstructing and compartmentalising the world; busily labelling and naming its constituent parts. It promises that when we finally uncover the basic building blocks of life we will be happy and content, with *meaning* assured. It has persuaded us to believe that everything is separate, not just human beings. All modern health care is based on this nutty premise. When there is no creator-type in the way - as is the case with our predominantly atheist, scientific pursuits - the liar has a great chance of filling those shoes; which it has done, easily.

None of this means that nothing good can come from science and it turns out that the detachment required for scientific pursuit is most effective in rationalising and reasoning our way into understanding our biggest problem. Ironically, without a detached and dispassionate approach to truth we are easily led into nonsense again by the liar. One of the first steps along the road to peace of mind is to stop taking offence. Only the liar in the mind can take offence, terrified of losing its status and being revealed. Once this reaction and denial technique has been undone, we are able to look more clearly at our madness, seeing it for what it is. Once we are unlikely to take offence at the idea we might be wrong, our biggest failings might be addressed.

The liar is our overarching divinity in these secular and scientific times. Its ideas and beliefs are reasonable and commonplace. It assures us that our body reigns supreme. Whenever the body reigns supreme, we may justify the destruction of faulty ones, be it by aborting foetuses that could *possibly* have a physical or mental disability at birth or by eliminating the sick in Nazi Germany.

And look at what happens when we do the liar's bidding and are supremely successful, utilising opportune circumstances and resources like those that were afforded Hitler not that long ago. Even then it is not satiated, insisting on more and more devastation; not to stop until everything is nothing. Be clear, the liar leads even its most loyal servants to doom. From deep within these situations, we believe we are the winners; but this is total madness because there is no winning in self-destruction, unless we have already agreed that self-destruction is the goal.

For the Nazis, the chosen worse-thans - which was everyone apart from this genetic Aryan, apparently - required destruction. How far would they have taken this, we wonder? And will someone just as insane appear again one day, offering us an even more disturbing example of what we are all capable? These are the effects of the liar's thought formula. We might even scientifically predict them given adequate circumstances, number of people in the group and resources required, as well as a necessary belief in overarching superiority that is stuck like superglue in the group mentality.

What a split in identity is fomented by the liar's ideas! These human beings - our brothers and sisters - believed that other human beings were less human than they. The psychosis generated by such a false belief is very painful, and the denial required for maintaining the lie brings even more agony. We can never dehumanise another without suffering ourselves. This is a natural law of the universe and easy to see. If we intentionally hurt a fellow, we are hurting ourselves. Furthermore, in truth, we would intentionally hurt a fellow *only* in order to hurt ourselves, because psychologically we live in total chaos, submerged in the absolute darkness of worse-than guilt; even when we are unemotional and believe in our indubitable superior state.

The Nazis showed us the most intense and exaggerated identity split we have ever seen, and the most excessive of all the liar's activities to date. A dark example for us to use in order to never forget what may happen if we don't address our collective psychosis. We should be very clear that we can all go the same way if we allow the liar to persuade us. The Nazi actions should have ensured that this was the final time we allowed ourselves to get so crazy. However, of course - because we do not know about the liar in the mind and our psychological pathology - it was not the last horror by far.

If we don't start healing our species-wide diseased minds, how long will it be before another Hitler springs up to lead us all to oblivion again? Perhaps the next global megalomaniac dictator will be ordering the murder of lizards masquerading as humans, the decision as to who is a lizard dependent on whim alone. Now that's a scary thought, but a familiar picture. Let's be honest with ourselves for once; we have solved no problem, ever, and no matter how appealing finger pointing might be, the snowball of hate is rolling still, gathering in intensity and supporters, to this day.

Small notions of hatred and condemnation, of wishing our brother dead, may appear to have insignificant effects. And who among us would think that there was anything abnormal about these thoughts? Yet they are all abnormal because they are all completely unfounded. However, these thoughts and ideas pepper our days, relatively noticed, rarely questioned. At intensity, coming from personal or group suffering, we may be persuaded to act on these thoughts and do what we will eventually regret. We are told that these destructive actions will save us from our pain, but they don't. Instead, they make the pain worse, more intense, so we act more destructively, more violently, and more aggressively in the hope we'll save ourselves this next time. However, we are never saved by destruction and the insane process of attempting to do so can spiral out of control with ease.

We all understand ourselves to be lacking something. We all feel, deep down, terribly guilty about how we view ourselves and our brothers, against the blinding truth to the contrary that we exhaust ourselves in suppressing. We are easily persuaded by the liar that we are better than the others. This belief, we assure ourselves, will make us feel better, more able to cope with this hellish existence. Thus, we race and compete, and build systems and organisations based on winning perceptual bouts. We collect qualifications and amass trinkets, all because we are terribly fearful. These activities, the liar promises, will assail our fear. We are all subject to this trickery and when the lie is shared by members of a labelled group, its seduction becomes much more powerful and so the defence it requires can grow into titanic proportions, becoming untouchable. Yet, we all do the same. We are all tempted toward the unthinkable in the hope that it might solve our deeper problem.

The actions of the Nazis and the tacit support of the German population, unsurprisingly, invoke harsh reactions and bitter vengeance in the hearts of survivors and onlookers alike. But acts of vengeance are no different from the acts inciting them and therefore solve no problem. Vengeance can be described as dehumanizing the dehumanizers who had already dehumanized themselves by their dehumanizing activities - because what we do to another we do to ourselves - and in doing so we ourselves become dehumanized. There are no winners here and any triumph or victory against evil oppressors is short lived and does not bring our loved ones back or erase the memories of past horrors.

The behaviour of those who have become insane to the degree that they can justify outrages against their fellow humans are what we might expect of an ape, suddenly and unexpectedly receiving the conscious capacity that humans enjoy. This ape would put his fear of predators into one new form, his fear of starving into another, his territorialism into another, and his desire for better-than-ness and ownership of the females into yet another. Yes, the liar is an evolutionary matter and we have been stuck at monkey-mind for way too long now. We are barely out of the swamp. Evolutionary theory sits well with our description of the liar but, contrary to the arrogance of cold, atheist scientists, the evolutionary process we are talking about here has not ended and is about to take a new, loving, and compassionate step.

When we calmly witness the liar in our own minds, as well as in the collective mind, we have arrived at the peace of mind required for viewing the liar dispassionately. And this is the only way to witness the liar safely. Sensitive souls, aware of its activities at intensity, while remaining in its stranglehold, usually become imbalanced by the experience. As we pick it apart, discarding one lie after another, never wondering if anything we find might be true, we realise that this liar that has had control of the human mind for eons is nothing at all. It doesn't, in fact, exist, because all of it is false. Yet while we are its sleepy willing allies, it will cause us to justify the inconceivable. The most intense expression of the insanity of the human race is surely the cold and calculated extermination of millions of people, simply due to their religious labelling.

We must forgive the Nazis because they are just another example of how we would all behave under the same circumstances and given a bitter, shared hatred of another person or group of people that we find ourselves having some *power over*. Furthermore, the German people must also forgive themselves their past for the same reason, the guilt of which is never far from the surface. The considerable shame remaining in the psyche of the German people ensures the necessary healing through self-forgiveness has not yet taken place.

If we don't forgive, and forgive properly, this will happen again. Maybe the next time it happens, that nuclear nightmare will be unleashed. In any case, actions caused by our shared worse-than/better-than complex are happening constantly, albeit in smaller, less grisly forms. The Nazis are surely the most extreme example we have given ourselves of the liar's capabilities. We can put this to beneficial use by noticing firstly, how far we can go, and secondly, how we would all do the same thing in the same position, and thirdly, how our forgiveness practice recognises these events as the inevitable effects of our species-wide insanity. When we are ready to accept that we have a problem, only then will we be able to do something effective about it. Until then, we can expect business as usual from the liar in the mind.

18 ISRAEL PALESTINE

We can see the process of evolution operating in two directions. In one direction, consciousness has taken new and varying material forms, over millions of years; from simple cellular structures, to water born creatures, to plants and animals on land; until it reached the form of the human being. With the human being's potential, consciousness is finally able to communicate, to relate and to understand why it is doing so. The human being is the only material life form on the planet that has the capacity to understand the conscious process.

Awareness pushes ever onwards towards the light of knowledge; from the quietness of the deep dark waters of the swirling oceans; then bravely onto land to breathe air, but remaining close to the safe cover of the cold water; then as plants, insects, and animals, sharing light and darkness under the sun and moon. Most recently, the evolution of consciousness produced the human being, as far as has been reached on this journey not yet complete. At each step of the way, fear was discarded to make room for more love and compassionate communication, even if it was just a tiny bit. We don't see ancient insect forms cuddling their young, but even these unusually constructed beings might be considered loveable by a mind that is able to look past appearances. This is the human mind.

In the other direction, the light of conscious awareness reaches down and pulls us ever closer towards it. There is much further to go on this journey; we are nowhere near the end of the road yet. The human being may realise that, on arrival at this place to which we have been travelling for eons, or even by simply accepting its existence, everything we believe we lack is immediately replenished. Until we see this, we will feel like strangers in a strange land. In moments of calm reflection, we are sure we do not belong here, in this world of fear and dread. This is true, we don't.

We are born and we quickly learn fearfulness. We arrive full of joy and, at the earliest opportunity, our light is put out by the liar. We know that what we have made of the world is a chaotic mess. We are aware that we do not like the world, even though we are compelled to protect it, cherish it, and so keep it going. Our deep sense of loneliness and loss is the empty space where the light of peace, love, and knowledge should be instead. Even so, we are not going to fail in our journey to the next step. The only thing we might do is waste time getting there. In fact, the only thing we are guilty of is time-wasting, and our potential for that is astronomical.

The liar tells us we are a single body, pitted against the whole universe. It notices our loneliness and desperation at this thought and so, due to the fear of discovery, it backtracks, persuading us that by owning the bodies of others, we will feel better, our fearfulness eradicated. On taking up ownership of a body, our fearfulness does seem to dissipate temporarily, even though any perception of ownership always blocks true communication with those we believe we own or are owned by. Nonetheless, because we sense we have benefitted by following the liar's orders, we feel secure in accepting its full range of mad edicts.

Anyone we believe we own is someone we have perceived as unworthy of the label *person*, or deserving the same rights we enjoy. On the other hand, if we believe ourselves *owned* by another, we will suffer more severe self-esteem issues. These roles are apt to change in the blink of an eye, and back again, but one role is usually more durable and pronounced than the other for longer periods. Subtly, in close relationships, this insanity is played out in the conditional love scenario, where peace is only achievable when people are behaving as we expect them to. In less subtle situations, we are able to justify all kinds of harsh treatment upon the bodies we believe we own. I used to get angry at my dollies when I was six. The poor things received some extremely violent treatment. Do you remember doing something like that with your body-representing toys too?

We believe that we are a body alone and that by owning another body or bodies our winning status, our salvation, will be assured. Even so, the underlying truth of our non-physical conscious connectivity is never too far from the surface, although the liar orders we ignore awareness of it. Nonetheless, no matter how much we deny the truth of our communion, this truth - without fail - informs our experience of the world. Because there is no separation, we too must suffer, whenever we hurt anyone.

We look to the external world we believe is real and important, away from the conscious communication we have with all life on Earth, and see more bodies and things that we might own and become happy by doing so. This ownership will, apparently, fill our deepest void. The liar tells us to amass whatever we can to save ourselves and we follow its orders with great enthusiasm. We may see that others are suffering by our actions, but this simply adds to our desire for more. We are so insane we do not realise that by depriving another, we ensure our own self-deprivation. We do not see our madness, even when we imperil the most obvious of shared resources, like the cleanliness of our water or the toxicity of the air we breathe.

The list of things that count as own-able extends outwards, becoming as unlimited as there are things to be owned. Even abstract notions of worldly knowledge are given importance in terms of who owns them. Land, of course, is no different. In fact, the ownership of land is one of the most bitterly disputed liar ideas there has ever been and so one of its favourites.

The belief in the right to own land started way back, before humans had appeared. It is another of the deeper evolutionary lies we believe, as it permeates through nearly all animal behaviour. This belief did not have to take on such complicated stories as we shifted from ape to human behaviour. The territorial wars of the apes have morphed into the fierce defence of personal space and frenetic acquisition of living space and land. Male cats spraying their local environment correspond directly to the stamping of documents that declare ownership of a house, for example.

Certainly, due to our unchecked and unexamined warring, aggressive, and violent natures, it makes sense to protect ourselves from that which we undoubtedly believe we are; that which wouldn't think twice about taking what was ours, our toys, our jobs, our food, our homes, our women, our clean water, our oil. That all these beliefs supporting violence are lies is a marvellous truth but, in the meantime, while we believe them, how could we behave any other way than with violence and war, assuming aggressive protective behaviour is a natural law.

This is how we all are; regardless of what labels define us and where we live. Our willingness to violently defend our belongings, or grab the belongings of someone else in a similar manner, may be less intense for us than it is for the next person, but we all have these beliefs at the core of our mental processes and everything we think and do is informed by them. Whether we are grabbing land unlawfully, or not returning a borrowed item, or using a tea bag three times, the deeper fear causing such unconscious actions is exactly the same. The fundamental shadowy liar idea is that we will be left with nothing if we don't act to protect ourselves.

We believe that the state of *now* is eternal. However, the state of things is not eternal; it is fleeting, temporary, and never worth killing or dying for. One year we might be the winner, but at some point in the future we will undoubtedly be the loser. Nothing stays the same forever in the material world. Ironically, now is the closest we do get to the eternal. The eternal *now* the mystics speak of is not so mystical. This *now* is obvious to a clear mind that has removed the obstacle of lies that blind us. This mind rests peacefully in the present moment, watching the madness around itself detachedly, and understanding the temporary nature of all things in the world. From this present moment perception, that which understands the illusory nature of everything we hold to be true, flows love and compassion. It is this state of mind alone that might heal our tired, sick world of devastation by providing effective plans of action.

The Israel-Palestine land issue is a terrible shame; mostly because those most recently persecuted by the liar's best effort to date have taken the role of persecutor. This is a pity indeed but, again, inevitable under the liar-mind scenario, from which no-one is free. I have said before, the liar doesn't take sides and who it has doing its bidding at intensity at any given moment is an arbitrary matter. The liar ensures that its bidding is being done but it doesn't care by whom. Those with a past full of suffering born of the insanity of the human race may shift focus at any moment, finding themselves in the position of abuser instead of victim; as we all will hate and love our nearest and dearest, changing our minds about them, moment to moment.

We have noticed that the abused become abusers, and the oppressed become oppressors, the owned become owners, and to and fro, backwards and forwards, reflecting the fleeting, temporary, and contrary nature of the dualistic world as we know it. These shifts must take place because none of us has understood the problem and so been able to arrest this perpetual motion. When fear remains unhindered, it may take gruesome forms. Of course, Israeli helicopter gunships bullying little boys throwing stones doesn't compare to the systematic slaughter of millions of people due to their religious status, but they are nonetheless both dehumanising acts. We should bear in mind what random attacks by thugs on the street might become, given sufficient organisation, manpower, and finance; as the Nazis proved to us.

If the pictures on the news give us anything of value, it is the proof that none of us are outside the liar's dominion of humanity, regardless of our level of perceived better-than-ness. In any case, any label of better-than comes from the liar itself, and so is always untrue. The truth is that, underneath this lie, is a deep sense of worthlessness and loss. The liar offers us freedom from the pain of the human mind struggling with its evolutionary baggage, and we accept its offer, not realising what might happen for having done so.

As we mentioned before, the intensity of our superiority complex reveals the level of our bad feelings about ourselves; those feelings lying not so far from awareness. If we have behaved very destructively in our lives and hurt a great many people - without having looked at our mind, noticed our madness, and forgiven ourselves for it - we will have a deep sense of personal pain that we will need to hide if we are to operate semi-normally in the world. The liar offers us this covering, but its gift is a Trojan horse and brings us no peace at all. Instead, any belief in better-than needs constant reinforcement because it cannot be true. Thus, our behaviour becomes even more unhelpful, our actions become even more destructive, cold and calculating, and everyone in the world suffers from our error in perception.

Let's not fool ourselves, better-than is a label that both sides believe they have. Each side believes in its better-than status, regardless of who has the most resources or firepower or land or whatever. Furthermore, each side points to the other and labels it worse-than. There is no definitive better-than; there cannot be, because we are all equal. The dreadlocked squatters are better than the police. Middle class home-owners are better than benefit claimants. Manchester United supporters are better than those supporting Arsenal. The Palestinians are better than the Israelis. And the Israelis are better than the Palestinians. It is all temporary, unfixed, changing with the wind; and it is all completely untrue. The truth is we are all optimally and divinely peaceful, and if we had the tiniest inkling of that our behaviour would change accordingly.

However, the liar mind rules and has us believing we are far from wonderful, even when it already persuaded of our indisputable better-than-ness. Our actions supply us with enough guilt to ensure we never see our true nature. Better-than, worse-than labels become so prominent in the collective mind during conflicts like that in the Middle East, the liar may invent more ways to persuade us to destroy our own bodies. If it can convince a toddler to smash his favourite toys up when he doesn't get what he wants, it can convince a grown adult to destroy his own body in an intense act of vengeance and desperation.

Each side in this conflict, as in any other, must forgive the other. Forgiveness means first arriving at the unquestionable conclusion that we are all the same; that there is no-one worse than or better than us; that when a person behaves spectacularly unhelpfully, it is because he is not in his right mind at the time and has no idea what he is doing. His behaviour is inevitable given the lies he believes and the intensity of suffering in his own heart. We extrapolate the reasoning into labelled groups too. From here we may see that everyone is doing the only thing they believe will alleviate their fearfulness.

I'm not here to offer solutions to complicated political issues but I do know that when we are able to love ourselves truly, and so love our brothers and sisters in the same way, all the decisions we make will necessarily bring us peace and joy. True love is the knowledge that there is no separation and that all labelling is bogus. I believe peace and joy is what we all want, no matter how twisted and distorted our thinking has become. Each side must forgive the other as each of us must forgive our brothers and sisters and ourselves.

We may forgive the Israelis for their actions based on fear of attack coming from all sides; the likely effects of a collective post-traumatic stress disorder. From this insecurity comes harsh defence in the form of attack, as per the liar's belief system. We forgive them their aggression and bullying based upon an overwhelming belief in their better-ness when compared to their neighbours. We may forgive the Palestinians for their actions based on fear of attack coming from all sides. The deep insecurity generated by intense hostility from their technologically advanced neighbours provokes harsh defence in the form of attack, as per the liar's foundations. We forgive them their desperate attempts to withstand the profound and unjustified loathing hurled at them, reset the balance and become less fearful in the process.

In the end, it is impossible to own land; the notion is the liar's perceptual construct. Home is where we are safe and protected. Home cannot be Israel or Palestine, whoever we are. Home will never be a place on Earth. Our true home is a perfected and still state of mind. Home is Heaven.com and nowhere else will suffice.

19 INTERNATIONAL TERRORISM

We all think we know what terrorism is; but do we? Let's try to be clear about this for once. The dictionary definition is as follows: the use of violence and threats to intimidate or coerce, especially for political purposes; the state of fear and submission produced by terrorism; a terroristic method of governing or resisting a government. Nowhere in this definition is any particular group singled out in order to set an example. Furthermore, nowhere in the definition does it mention that certain groups may dodge the label *terrorist* when they behave in this way. Nevertheless, we humans believe that terrorist acts are justified - and so avoid the definition - when we ourselves are behind them. This madly erroneous belief is founded entirely on the certainty that we are better than the rest of humanity who, therefore, do not deserve the same treatment we expect for ourselves.

We in the West believe terrorists come from faraway places, intent on robbing us of our highly superior way of life. These terrorists, we believe, are *evil* and condemnable; they should rot in hell. When dissatisfaction within our own boundaries reaches extremes, and similarly enraged folk rise up from among us to murder their fellows, we believe this sort of terrorism to be the exception. We believe home-grown terrorism to be anomalous; an outlier in the set of terrorist activities we are aware of which are usually committed, we believe, by very *evil*, foreign - usually dark-skinned - people who hate us and covet what we have worked so hard to amass.

The label with which we stamp a terrorist group usually signifies an underlying patriotism towards a country or racial label. Of course, patriotism is a liar-device and one for which we are convinced it is reasonable to die. How could we have become mad enough to assume this idea is reasonable and sane? This, again, is part of our evolutionary hangover which brought territorialism and the fear of loss of home into the human experience as we morphed from wilder, more savage, simian forms. Bizarrely, this fear of losing the ownership of home and territory is limited entirely to personal and group land ownership, while we now observe as a species, mostly disinterestedly, our shared home approaching a state of unfitness for life as we know it; another solid proof of human insanity.

Patriotism is reasonable and normal in the human perception under the liar; a perception in which the importance of perceived differences is paramount. Members of the group we belong to are given more value over others. From here we can justify atrocities against those others, the worse-thans, the non-members of our special group. If there could be anything useful about this lie, it might be a shift into overprotectiveness for the planet on which we all live. A global patriotism, although still based on separation, could generate the effective problem solving strategies we desperately need for the environmental and social issues looming over us. But it could only arise from a firm and incontestable belief in the equal value of every human being.

Patriotism gives us a team to belong to. We feel safe and secure; special members of a special club. However, underneath the flag waving, cheering, and indulgence in life-stories of people we have never met, is fear. We believe our group must be protected from attack and so, to avoid the inevitable, we attack first and with impunity, wherever we deem it necessary. The bigger the bully we are, the more safe and secure we will be, we believe. In the last few decades we have witnessed too many instances of colossal bullying all over the world; civilian jets brought down for no good reason, illegal wars, pre-emptive strikes (which simply means *we started it*), lies and subterfuge in the media in order to mould public acquiescence, and failure by politicians to justify wars after the fact. Do any of us actually feel safer or more secure? The answer is no; indeed less so, the chaos and devastation continuing to this day, wherever we have involved ourselves under false pretences.

The older generation tend to take a rosy and fake view of the past, believing it to have been far better than what we have now. They bore us with repeated lists of all the amazing things our country has done and how great it is. Oftentimes, there is a conjunct sermon going on about how bad everyone else is when compared to our great and better-than nation. Curiously, patriotism can become so deranged that we become convinced that everything good and useful that has ever existed was invented by our own special group of people.

We would be more than happy to martyr ourselves for this special club to which we belong. We dream of the pomp of war and how important we would be if we were to lay down our pathetic little lives for our glorious country. Like everything else in our world, the most insane notions are given credence and reasonability, even though proof of the truthful opposite stares us constantly in the face. Our selective memory skips over the waste of millions of young lives - snuffed out in arguments over a few metres of land in the First World War - focusing instead on the fake splendour and triumph while remaining blind to the madness of dumb duty to better-than leaders.

Patriotism is the same old separation-psychosis given yet another ugly form in the human world. It is inevitable that one human group should pit itself against another and it is always nonsensical. In reality, the liar has no real favourites, no matter how convinced we are that we are the best of the bunch. The liar is just a thought processing machine after all and doesn't actually have a personal opinion. Its function is to split apart and destroy and, to this end, it uses the weapons in which we invest, rewarding us with the billions earned on their sales. Patriotism is the liar's marvellous invention with which it seduces otherwise normal people, just like you and me, into reverting to savage behaviour normally limited to far older forms of life on Earth.

Patriots must defend themselves. Anyone who isn't part of the special group will potentially be an enemy; out to get us, attack us, and take what is ours. For this reason, terrorist-type activities are often deemed justifiable in order to protect the group from the inevitable attacks coming from outside. Notice that this situation is no different from the fear a single person has of his perceived vulnerability and the measures he may take in order to mitigate it. At the governmental level, this belief in group vulnerability, and the fear generated by it, encourages the most abhorrent attack and defence strategies; a lot of it hidden in the shadows, away from anyone sane enough to question it. Furthermore, there is no government in the world that has not had its hands in the dirtiest business of espionage and terrorism; some more than others, usually dependent on resources available.

Unlike the Nazis, who had perfected the liar's world to the extent that they were able to be reasonably open about their appalling enterprise, the terrorist operates in obscurity. Rarely known personally by those ministerial advisers and government officials that request illegal action behind closed doors, these groups can be relied upon, for the right money, to do the dirtiest work of politics; the assassinations, the bombings of innocent civilians in peacetime, the ethnic cleansings in illegal wartime, the blackmailing of party leaders and royalty, the smuggling of drugs and radioactive material which has the potential to destroy the world, to name but a few examples of what our governments get up to on our behalf.

The lies underpinning the shady political level of the human world are unquestionable by those who support and act upon them. That the majority of the good citizens of their countries would not be able to make similar justifications is conveniently overlooked in favour of the liar's mad bellowing. Officials whose minds have become so unhinged - where personal power or blind deference to the group's ideals has become more important than life itself - are convinced their actions are of value, necessary, and justifiable. Lofty self-identities are bound up in the lunacy of responsibility for unnecessary deaths. Very insane people are running our world, making disastrous political decisions that affect everyone. And we would do the same in their shoes. It is no wonder that the world is in such chaos.

Like the media and the ad men, the officials and advisers that employ terrorists to arrange their duplicitous goals understand very well how the liar functions. They know what pleases it, what displeases it, how to manipulate a mind under its control, and what might terrify such a mind beyond belief. They know all this with no knowledge of what the liar in the mind is. With the most fundamental of the liar's ideas held as conscious and reasonable beliefs, where might these people draw the ethical line?

Manipulating the labelling process is something that only the liar knows how to do efficiently. It knows exactly how someone defining themselves by a particular label will react when this label is threatened. It understands exactly how to persuade a rigid thinker, loyal to its label, into attacking first. The liar's manipulation can be very subtle and permeates all levels of human experience. When we start to notice our own liar-based thoughts, we are surprised to see we have been tricked so efficiently, and for so long, with simple concepts and ideas alone. If our allies are cruel and selfish liar-mind-devices, we could spend our lives manipulating labels and beliefs for our own ends. We might feel at home working in advertising, marketing, and PR roles. When we are particularly smart, or if we have gone to the right school, we might find ourselves working for the secret service of our countries in a similar capacity.

At the personal level, we play petty power games with each other, using the information we have about people, places, and the situations we know. We believe that we are the winner when we have more information than the others. Perhaps we are very proud to be able to say with confidence which restaurant or hotel is the best. Our sense of personal pride (better-than) gets out of control when we gossip maliciously about another person. At the level of international politics, we might find that ownership of information designated important brings us leverage in the political arena. Perhaps we could sell it for millions too. Or maybe we should hold onto it instead, assured of its powerfulness at the appropriate time.

We cherish and protect the knowledge we own in exactly the same way as we do our bodies, money, and land, and we defend it as fiercely under threat. In the most extreme liar-invented situations - the dark corridors of political power and the terrorist cells waiting for the call - we rarely see who the winner is. Yet those who hold the power, the knowledge, the finances, and resources believe themselves to be the winners, whether it is open to view or not. We might reason that whoever the winner is at any given time shifts constantly from one side to another, just like it does in our personal relationships. The belief in fearsome enemies can never be subdued in the group mind, just as the belief in the existence of personal enemies never disappears entirely from our singular minds.

It is not too difficult to see how an extremely psychotic mind might believe dark forces are out to kill its body, or make its life impossible in some way, given that such a thought is a common theme coming from the liar we have allowed to control our minds. Furthermore, it is not too difficult - in the other direction - to see how this psychosis may justify the killing of other bodies in order to save ourselves from certain destruction. A deeply fearful mind can lose control of reason and begin to imagine that all sorts of bad things are about to happen. The intense imbalance of such a mind allows it to perceive the illusion that people and groups are determined to cause it some harm. This belief is so strong it is constantly proven by its projection into the external world.

This is the paranoid thinking that we all entertain at varying levels of intensity, but it can become pronounced in certain unfortunates who have experienced deeper and more enduring suffering. We could say that terrorist thugs, their leaders, and the countries and government officials that support them are simply the projected, organised forms of an extremely psychotic and paranoid group mind-space with which we are all personally familiar. There is no difference in the content of our fears; the form of their expression, however, knows little limitation. Paranoia might well be a requirement for admittance into such malevolent environments. And if it is not already apparent at entry, it will soon be acquired.

Terrorism and secret service activity are extreme forms of the paranoid beliefs dished up by the little puff of madness we all suffer from, the liar in the mind. Within the shady worlds of terrorism and espionage, legal systems are powerless, as is the public eye, in order that liar's most vicious and perverse game may avoid obstruction. Occasionally, we learn of the inhumanity of the officials that govern us, but most often knowledge like this is easily obscured by a celebrity scandal, or whatever. It may even be that the public of apparently *free* countries know less of their government's activities than those people living under dictatorships where, as with the Nazis, the murderous ideology need not be so hidden.

History is littered with skulduggery. It is a naïve and patriotic mind that believes that the people currently in power could not have done the nefarious things that certain voices suggest. A cursory look at the history books reveals one dastardly treachery after another, listed and catalogued, century after century, with no limits on the destruction of anyone or anything in the way of whoever was *all powerful* at the time. To believe that all this deviousness is limited to an epoch that ended around fifty years ago is decidedly insane and, if true, would suggest we had all found enlightenment and peace all of a sudden, which we clearly have not. It also insists on the better-ness of the race we believe would not do such things. We are far too good for that, we might insist, forgetting the bloodthirsty avarice of our colonialist ancestry and the like. The truth is that no-one has a monopoly on destructive blundering or hypocritical denial. We are all the same.

On the other hand, approaching the truth threatens the liar intensely and it will become extremely active under threat of discovery. When a smart enough soul starts to close in on it in earnest, it becomes sharply inventive and subversive, persuading us to point the finger more fervently and bitterly. The liar reshapes diligent truth-seekers into preposterous monsters in order that we might believe them to be irrational and unstable. The state of mind of those who have *nearly* noticed the liar is often as deranged as that which they are condemning. It is very difficult to take the subsequent circular arguments seriously. This cloaking activity assures business as usual for the liar in the collective consciousness.

Nevertheless, the trickery of which our governments are capable is beyond our comprehension, particularly as we have apparently put our trust in them. It is always painful to face up to the fact that our friends, our children, or our loved ones might be up to no good and we fear that, by accepting the truth about them, we too will *look bad* in the eyes of others. We stubbornly avoid the truth and the suffering continues. We would rather label our own child with *ADHD* and sedate him than admit there might be a bigger issue with our parenting. Accepting the criminality of governments shows the people, us, in a bad light. Better to ignore the stories we hear, putting them down to unhinged activists, hippies, and conspiracy theorists. That way we might maintain our better-ness. However, again, it is a naïve mind that believes acts of terrorism are restricted to those we are currently labelling *terrorists*. How did we miss noticing that these labels change and swap, to-ing and fro-ing with the wind, the once enemy now friend, the once friend now enemy, always dependent on whose back needs scratching or whose back is being scratched and, more likely, who is currently favoured by our god of profit.

The arms industry makes corporations and governments very wealthy indeed. As you might imagine, in a world in which conflict, violence, and aggression is an essential part of life, an arms trade easily becomes reasonable and justifiable, never questioned for sanity. The amount we spend on killing each other is astounding. We trouble-make, inciting conflicts in far-away places so that we may sell the guns we have made. We may even project manage the production and sales to war-torn countries, beginning manufacture long before unrest was even dreamt of by the local population. And how could it be any other way, given our insanity?

Yet, do we winners of this business think we are so safe, managing to circumvent suffering ourselves? Are the temporary profits made for government coffers and defence corporations worth all this bloodshed? Does the receptionist at the defence company believe she is not complicit in the devastation wrought in foreign places? Do we think we are not complicit ourselves, even though we personally aid the financing of the arms industries with our hard earned taxes?

Our governments are clearly not interested in our future. They are peopled by we who believe we are bodies alone and so going to die and that's that; and so while we're here on Earth we'd better do as well as we can in our careers, and get our hands on as much as we can and be the winners in every sense. We seem to believe we might take the items and status we achieve with us to nowhere when we die. We act as if all these vacuous goals make us happy, peaceful, and content. Wow; we are so mad and we have elected the maddest of us to make the key decisions that affect everything.

Regardless of how bad it has become, we must be compassionate and avoid the liar's temptation to angry reaction. Too many of us have the blood of innocents on our hands and this must be our focus. Terrorist acts are the most intensely impersonal form of the liar's goal. An order is given, no questions asked, and innocents die in revenge attacks and pre-emptive strikes, while people submit to the savage whims of dictators. The language of terrorism has even been twisted into vagueness and respectability. For example, the phrase, *winning hearts and minds*, coined to support an illegal war, became a euphemism for murder; the liar's work indeed. Terrorism has become a project management exercise that even has a linguistics department to hand.

We have convinced ourselves that war is a worthwhile goal. As children, we indulge ourselves in war games, cowboys and Indians, and the re-enactment of battles. Our mothers buy us toy guns and swords, and we run around with our playmates, imitating the ultra-violence we hear about in history class and see on the TV every night. As we grow up, our taste for aggression does not dissipate. Later on, perhaps, we find ourselves at the operating end of a gun, pointing and shooting, taking the lives of other human beings. We feel elation and ecstasy at finally achieving the goal we have dreamt of for so long. However, soon after, the depression sets in because we have also destroyed ourselves with our actions, even though we are not consciously aware of having done so.

The paid assassins that don't ask questions - they who never flinch as they cruelly annihilate innocent civilians, women and children - are ignorant of the motivations behind their mandates. We need to forgive these shadowy figures; these sad souls that can kill little children, up close and personal, for the money they make or an imagined brownie point from God. The mind of our brother who can justify all this is so wrecked, so chaotic, he cannot help but repeat his actions. So slathered is he with the dark, heavy slime of guilt, that making the decision to change his ways is unlikely. He is more probably destined to die in a similarly horrible manner at the hands of a fellow worker in the field. Perhaps this man or woman started out in their career with idealism and a passion for a patriotic or religious label of some sort. The liar's darkest activities will soon snuff out any wide-eyed enthusiasm.

Over time, while murder remains on the daily to-do list, the soldier and the terrorist must become colder, harder, and more firmly convinced of the nothingness of life; the liar's foundation. This will keep him going, although guilt will be building up subconsciously. Even a *religious* terrorist cannot escape the guilt arising from hurting his innocent brother, whoever his brother might be. His brother is himself, after all, and all his holy books will have mentioned this inescapable fact to him, on more than one occasion. He will focus on the minutiae of twisted religious messages and ignore their foundations in order to rationalise his activities. However, he will never forget the key spiritual points.

The mind of the terrorist that has lost any sense of peace may simply give up and accept damnation as a way of life. Perhaps this mind had never questioned anything; the power of better-than beliefs much stronger than common sense. Minds in the grip of this sort of madness are unable to consider a better way, even to the point of pulling the cord that will blow up the body housing them. The liar leads us inevitably to sickness and death. If we find a violent death along the road, far sooner than expected, so much the better. When we meet death by suicide, the liar is delighted. If we are to experience a *righteous* death at our own hands, we become the special guest at the liar's award ceremony in the sky.

How does the irrevocably broken terrorist fare in peace time; he who chases *peace* for his leaders the way they require it; *peace* redefined to mean occupation and the wanton destruction of all those who don't concur. Those who have only ever felt truly alive when firing a gun, how do they cope with the silence of no-war? How could they cope, they who believe that meaning and purpose come with the abhorrent abuses committed on innocent civilians?

This was the man who whooped and yelled in glee as he napalmed a small village full of women and their tiny children. He followed his orders to the letter. Not just from his superiors, but from the liar in his mind which naturally activates at intensity within violent conflict. When war is over, what then? Depression must come and the healers of our poor brothers - and there are healers available if one is sought - undertake the undoing of complicated perceptual knots to bring the mind back to an awareness of love. The healers that do this important work, of unravelling the liar in the mind of the terrorist and soldier, show us the compassion we may have for someone so profoundly wrecked by our tortured world. Healing is the beginning of the awareness of the inescapable responsibility we have for all life and healing is available for everyone, no matter how bad they have been.

Even so, many of us still believe that murder is a way of life, and thus of value. Yet, no matter what we believe, we cannot honestly enjoy a murderous life, and we cannot truthfully give it any value either. The reality is that we are divinely compassionate and peaceful human beings; that is the nature of the human being. To act as we have done is only possible when believing a fundamental lie about ourselves; that we are no good and worthless. We rarely notice our true nature, that which is all powerful in a very real sense. Instead, we permit ourselves to be driven to destruction, whipped into line, forced along by the liar in our minds; that which insists that weakness is strength and that we will only be happy by winning this pathetic game of *who's got the weakest mind?* Along the way, we deprive as many as we can, relabeling such deprivation as *protecting our interests*; these interests that we hate.

The thoughts we mentioned earlier - those we notice with horror, certain that they are not ours - are the thoughts and ideas we consider legitimate and reasonable in the midst of the insanity of war and terrorist acts. There is nothing sane or healthy about violence and I don't think anyone could argue that there is. Terrorism and war are the liar's playgrounds where it does not have to hold back or hide itself. Here, we witness the liar's core beliefs take form; on show, proudly worn by its hosts, like the medals consequently earned for obediently doing its bidding.

Terrorists operate inside and outside societies, for and against governments. Terrorist acts may be in support of a particular group, or a particular government, but sometimes we might see the most grisly business coming from a blatant hatred of those not deemed significant enough to deserve the right to life on Earth. As we uncover the liar in the collective perception, and begin assuring ourselves of our connectivity and loving togetherness, the truth about terrorist acts that we may have accepted as being the work of one person, or a particular terrorist group or country, will be revealed as the shady work of the governments we trusted. We may even see evidence of friend and enemy working together on the most horrendous of crimes against the innocent. We will find healing by accepting our complicity, by knowing that we would have done the same thing in the same situation as these shadowy unseen figures, their hands dripping in the blood of our families and friends.

No-one is free from the effects of international terrorism. Anything that may get in the liar's way, and in the way of its government sponsors, must be eradicated. Heart-breaking assassinations of the voices for peace within our societies, such as that of Martin Luther King or Gandhi for example, deliver more sad proof of our diseased collective mind. Anything at all that obstructs the liar's business is immediately earmarked for silencing. Furthermore, we should never forget that peace itself is an obstacle to the liar and its supporters, and therefore to us too. The peaceful must be abolished in order to maintain the liar's rule.

Each of us thinks our life is meaningful, even when we have mistaken meaning for experiences that have no meaning at all; nothingness, the vacuum of the liar's world. Yet this self-deception is the only way we will not question the liar every day, minute-by-minute, as we should be doing. If we knew that our beliefs alone have built our tortured world, we might start questioning them. Instead, we rest assured that there is value in our lives, even when we are severely discontent. The terrorist's life is the most intense example of this.

All this wanton destruction and no-one ends up with anything at all. What does anyone profit from illegal, spooky terrorist activities? Who profited from the assassination of Martin Luther King Jr., or Gandhi, or Jesus Christ and other similar spokespeople for peace. The answer is, no-one. Nothing is gained and everything is lost, just as the liar likes it.

Are we so fast asleep we don't see all this? And why, if we do see it, can we do nothing about it? The reason nothing can be done is because we attend to the effects without having squarely addressed the cause. The cause is the perceptual psychosis that all humans share. Once we start agreeing that our species is suffering this obvious problem, we might then be able to start changing our minds about each other and so move towards building a dependable, inclusive, and enduring peace on Earth.

When we can see we have been fooled, for so long, we might feel sorrow and remorse for a while. But this will be short-lived. Next, there might be an epoch of comedic laughter, in which we won't be able to believe we could have been as stupid as we are being now. Eventually, we will forget about these dismal times, the very last cycle in which the liar had total control of our minds. Its global dictatorship will become a vague memory, assigned to mythology. The idea that some people are better than others will seem as ridiculous as suggesting the moon is made of cheese.

As Martin Luther King, Jr. said: *A lie cannot live.*

20 WHEN BUDDHISTS MURDER MUSLIMS

Usually, we imagine the good Buddhist people to be the most peaceful among us. Compassion and care for all life is a fundamental requirement in Buddhism; unlike other world religions which may insist on compassion for humans but rarely for the natural world too. Children from Buddhist cultures start a meditation practice early on, and anyone sensitive to the energy of environments will notice a stillness in Buddhist countries that is not apparent in the frenetic, me-me-me surroundings with which we are more familiar in the West.

The Buddha certainly understood the human mind very well. He was the first to be clear about the temporary meaninglessness of the things we cherish in the world and, hence, its illusory nature. He was the first to lay out plainly the fact that the monkey-mind (a Buddhist term) controls our lives; he saw it as the loudest voice in our unexamined conscious processes, obstructing peace of mind, joy, and contentment. The meditation practices he formulated for ridding the mind of the liar's trash were very effective and today, nearly three thousand years later, we continue to use his techniques because they actually do work. Peace of mind resulting from meditation, which many of us are experiencing all over the world, is a no faith required exercise in proof by results.

The Buddha saw that the 'I' we believe defines us, is part of the illusory nature of the world. Moreover, it is this 'I' that sits most closely to the concept of *liar* we are discussing. However, Buddhists maintain that the problem of the human mind is hugely difficulty to overcome. They are certain that freedom from perceptual chains is achievable only after many, many lifetimes of serious practice. Personally, I'm not sure we have so much time on our hands. In any case, the Buddha did not explain our problem as arising from a single error, subsequently taking form in an unlimited number of ways. Nor did he see the problem extending into common group perceptions or the collective mind space in the way it has in our modern, interconnected times.

During meditation, we get a front row seat to the liar's tomfoolery. We become aware that its ridiculous ideas are not our own and recognise them for the nonsense that they are, refusing to believe them or act on their suggestion. The Buddha did not mention the liar in the mind and its nearly full control of the human thought processes or, if he did, we lost the simplicity of the message over the centuries, preferring to believe in the necessity of an intense and severe meditation practice from which hardly a handful of us have emerged successful. Many people, on their first attempts at Buddhist meditation, quit because it is so difficult.

Therefore, although a Buddhist may achieve much peace from meditation practices, unfortunately the liar is still pouncing around in the mind, and therefore liable to persuade him to believe the impossible again. Furthermore, he may still be seduced into defending his erroneous beliefs with violence and aggression. Sadly, even the peace-loving Buddhists are not free of the liar in the mind.

Recently we witnessed the unexpected scenes of Buddhists in Myanmar attacking and killing the Muslim people that share the country with them. These Buddhists have grown to hate the Muslims with the same fervour any one of us has when the liar persuades us there is one person, or a group of people, assuredly worse than ourselves. From here, annihilation by us better-thans may be justified. The relatively peaceful-minded, Buddhist people in Myanmar lost their cool and allowed the liar to take over, provoking murderous reactions. Moreover, remarkably, some of those on the rampage were monks and religious persons.

It is true that meditation brings a quietness of mind rarely experienced by more savage folk. From a calm mind, we make beneficial and selfless decisions. Yet, even Buddhism has not been able to halt the liar's activities that continually seduce us into believing in inequality between humans. This is in direct opposition to the tenets of Buddhism, and all those Buddhists that took part in the regrettable activities in Myanmar will be aware of this at some level. This is a huge split in identity and must have caused the people much inner turmoil and confusion.

All of us, without exception, are crashing around the world, causing as much destruction as the liar can generate. If we are not taking part in the madness ourselves, we will have been lulled to sleep in order that more efficient liar-based decision makers can get on with the devastation without interference. Even we sleeping ones spend our lives in bitter conflict with family and friends; every hateful word and action coming from deep and unexamined fearfulness. We don't see that any action based on fear, however miniscule, is a pebble in the pond that may set off that final tidal wave of destruction for which the liar salivates endlessly. If we are held to account for our outrages, we might insist we were just doing our jobs, just following orders. We have no idea who the boss is though.

Ever since we can remember, fear has been the keystone of our experience of life. The liar is the fearful thought construct we invented when we became aware of ourselves and were still very frightened monkeys. Today, millions of years later, none of us are yet free of the liar in the mind and whenever we cherish a lie, even a seemingly tiny one, the power of our erroneous belief is quickly put to chaos generation.

Nevertheless, what we know of reality is so limited, so small, to experience even the tiniest speck of truth changes us forever. From fear comes our disastrous world; from love will come the saving of it. However, given that the liar is running the show and no-one has a clue about it existence, even the most spiritual among us will be governed by its whims; often more obviously so than the non-spiritual among us.

The belief in the reality of fear, and the application of fearful practices in order to mitigate it, is the cause of all the unforgivables we have struggled so long to understand. Now we know of the liar in the mind, our fearful behaviour can be seen as inevitable and understandable, and therefore easy to forgive. However, anything that does not arise from love, in any period, is unjustifiable. The liar's slippery mind trick persuades us to ignore, condone, and excuse atrocities from behind the façade of a spiritual life without having first understood how they could have happened. We will always struggle with the convoluted and problematic definitions of freedom doled out to us by the liar.

When we insist that all our behaviour has been reasonable, at all times, because we believe we are now at peace in a spiritual sense, we are hypocrites. While we in the West have stopped stoning women for trivial matters, many parts of the world have not yet caught up and still do not find these actions unacceptable. While the world remains insane, we should make sure that accepting things as they are never includes an insistence on the reasonability of the behaviour, whenever and wherever it may have taken place. If we believe that the appalling acts of the past were reasonable because at the time people were too ignorant to know any better, we have completely missed the point and failed to pick up on the liar's trickery.

Ignorance is never an excuse and is its own reward indeed. Things were as they were, but it never makes them OK. Remember, one error is the same as any other and anything that supports fear is unjustifiable, however small it may seem to be. Allow just one error into the pot of reasonability and reason vanishes and we open the floodgates to the most frantic expressions of insanity. This is exactly what happens when religious cults get out of control and start to brazenly condone the unthinkable. Usually, the leaders want to uphold one aspect of fearfulness. However, keep one tiny bit of fear, and you keep the lot; the nature of the hologram.

There is a huge difference between accepting what *is* and condemning it, and accepting what *is* and condoning it, but neither of these approaches are away from liar-mind rule. As humans having a spiritual experience, we have become confused enough to think that one of these false protocols is reasonable given that it appears to be the opposite of the other. However, the Nazi's actions will never be OK and we will never sing Nazi songs again cheerfully. The actions of men who believe that women and girls are available to own and used for sex will never be OK, and we will never sing those paedophile pop songs again without wincing.

One day, soon hopefully, young people will watch a film such as The Wolf of Wall Street and not become hypnotically enthralled by a good-looking, drug-crazed, womanising thief, and start planning an imitation of him as their life's ambition; and those reactions came from the teenage girls I spoke to! We must look back at our madness and vow to never repeat it, by understanding it as madness. Looking at the liar and finding examples like these serves us well by proving unequivocally how we have all been fooled into believing destruction is a worthy goal; all of us; particularly when it is given an enticing, Hollywood gloss. With no notion of the liar in the mind, we remain completely blind.

If one instance of fear remains justified, while the others not, we are hypocrites. It is never reasonable to vent rage on a group of people we have judged loathsome because we are never responsible for the judgment. But the liar's deception reigns supreme when it manages to incite attack on other groups based on a comparison of religious practices. If we believe it is OK to kill people because they are not as peaceful, loving, or equanimous as we are, we have hit the big time in hypocrisy.

The Myanmar atrocities are a useful illustration of the intensity of our insanity and the extent of the liar's control of the human species. They show, unequivocally, that even when we are outwardly aligned with peaceful ideals, we may slip up and label our brother non-human and so condone his murder. This is even possible from religious leaders whose apparent main tenet and daily sermon is peace and love.

We must forgive the monks and the people of Myanmar for their insanity because it is insanity. We forgive ourselves at the same time as a side effect. We ask the Myanmar Buddhists to forgive their Muslim brother for whatever charges they hold against him. We ask them to remember their sanity and the fact that all humans are equal and deserve the same compassionate treatment. We remind them that whatever their problem was, their reaction to it has saddened the youthful first buds of the sane and loving world.

21 BIEBER

I'm absolutely sure that dear young Justin Bieber is a lovely lad and has been very good to his mum over the years. The poor boy has simply had the misfortune of becoming one of the most famous celebrities in the world. This has clearly wrecked his head a little and, as the liar is in charge of all worldly proceedings, ours too. We love him and we hate him, oftentimes with unnecessary fervour. Indeed, if we have an opinion, we are polarised when it comes to the world's most recent goofy heartthrob. Some of us adore him to the point of believing he is our own personal property, while others of us would rather murder him.

Wee Justin rules the mind of the teenage girl that adores him. He recently received the accolade of *third-most powerful celebrity in the world*; bizarrely, Forbes Magazine considers the whims of teenage girls as having some power, although I hardly think they could be mobilised into doing any serious harmfulness. Reasonably insipid, the most harm Justin has done is in convincing millions of adolescent females that devotion to his divine-like, celebrity status is a valid pastime and worth every penny of pocket-money. Is this why he gets the rest of us so riled up? If so, we will have assumed that if we too happened to be young, female, and desperate for the love of a boy, there is no way we would be mad enough to focus every minute of our thinking time on this lad. But this is simply not true; we would all fall into the same trap given the same circumstances; as we would also fall into the same trap of celebrity, if we were unlucky enough to find ourselves in the great lord Justin's position.

In five years, this pretty young whippersnapper has taken over the world, apparently. And whether we love him or hate him, our shared consciousness is full of him. And whatever foolish lewdness he acts out to please his devotees would be no different from any other teenage boy's behaviour, given the same resources and opportunity. In fact, his mouth has been far cleaner than those of most boys his age; as any school teacher will assure you.

Bieber firms up our belief in the importance of bodies and physical appearance. His presence confirms the liar's main tenet, that the body is supreme and very valuable. He seduces us into indulging the liar's requirement to own others bodies, alive or dead. He assures us that the ownership of his body is possible, as proven by all young girls hanging a picture of him on their wall. He is one of those irrelevant celebrities whose life stories we believe to be more important than *real* news; proven by the fact that people are more interested in pathetic stories about his bad behaviour than those of toddlers being bombed in Iraq, for example. Riches are guaranteed to any network running the Bieber story in place of the suicide bomber report. This is a sad fact of our world, and none of this is particularly insidious either. The god of profit rules us all and, while it does, we would all choose money over life.

Nevertheless, it won't be too long before these zombified schoolgirls replace their Bieber idol with a real *love* affair. And, undoubtedly, it won't be too long before another young punk will step into his shoes to hypnotise today's toddlers and perplex the cynics. I'd actually never heard of him until recently; that is perhaps one of the blessings of living a little ways off the grid. I began to see his name in bitter rants on Facebook, and the like, and so wondered what all the fuss was about. It all seems hardly worth worrying about, as it is just nonsense. But, at the same time, it is a wonderful proof of our lack of sanity.

It has been many a long year since I have stepped into a high street fashion outlet and didn't immediately feel some mental distress coming from the music blaring in my ears. Squawking singers reconstituted into metallic twanging; drumbeats pounding into the skull like pneumatic drills; screeching two-note melodies my cat renders better; the music scene today has become a sure representation of hell. Indeed, the modern music scene is an appalling representation of the vacuum, another projection of the liar's hellish reality we all now consider normality onto the mind-space media of music. Aggressive, iniquitous, and banal messages incite uber-violence and coma; but if that is what our everyday thoughts contain anyway, we will fail to notice anything unusual. Bieber fits in well in this world, even though his lyrics contain corny puppy love references rather than *fuck the hoes*; perhaps he's working up to that.

Filling our heads with the drivel that passes itself off as music these days is the same as being highly addicted to Valium; we drift into a perceptual sleep, subject to the constant drone of nothingness that keeps us vacant, zombie-like, and unable to act decisively. Like nails driven into the skull, we subject ourselves to this idiocy day after day; all day at work, in the car, at the office, cooking dinner, constantly. The music industry, like every other - and let's not forget we are talking about a corporate environment again - is controlled entirely by the liar.

The liar knows very well what pleases the minds it resides in and, for the last half century or so, we have been inventing Justin Biebers that appeal to hysterical teenage girls; those who have, most interestingly, become the loudest and most desperate voices crying out for love. They mistakenly believe that the love they have noticed is very much lacking can be found in the worship of pop idols. And, as the money starts to roll in, we are unable to question the meaning or validity of our moronic enterprise. There must also be a million wannabe Biebers out there; doing their thing, day in, day out, waiting for their big break. Justin was the lucky one, apparently, although a life like his could barely be an experience of living. This is easy to see when we are examining the situation rationally.

The human world as we know it offers us a short, meaningless void with a guarantee of death at the end. Every year that goes by, as we become more closely interconnected, more examples of our faith in death by worship of the body, and thus meaninglessness, swoop down on us from the music industry in the form of pretty young boys, scantily clad girls, and violent black male sex addicts. You didn't notice that? As fans, we either want to be just like them or own their bodies. We have no idea who our fellow humans are, nor do we care to know. These lies believed give some meaning to our dreary lives. We are all beliebers.

But are we really so incensed by this young boy? Really? Or is it more that we are fed up with the manufactured lifestyles that seduce our youngsters? Is Bieber a model for what we all would like to become while the liar runs the world and we're jealous we're not him? Does he represent the winner? If so, we must be lunatics. Does our swinging from love to hate of this boy-child - he that is in no way any more special than any other - signify our profound insanity, unchecked and unnoticed? Or do we hate him so much because we subconsciously realise that what he supports is an appalling waste of our time?

In truth, there is nothing to love and nothing to hate about the Justin Bieber idol and if we have allowed ourselves to be distracted by this nothingness, we are just wasting our time. And there is no need for us to time-waste a second longer. Let's instead begin the process of healing our beleaguered minds of every nightmare that pretends to be a valid dream.

22 MY BEST FRIEND

Often, the most *spiritual* among us appear to be the most intolerant. Organised religion has certainly played its part in atrocities over the centuries and even today. Many of us believe we know what forgiveness means and are practicing it successfully. Those of us that are working on a forgiveness practice might have some success here and there, but picking and choosing what to forgive is not what forgiveness is about. The ability to forgive some things and not others reveals ignorance as to why we cannot help but behave the way we do. For this reason, condemnation still seems appropriate for particular cases of the *unforgivable*. Moreover, often, that which we are continuously unable to forgive is the most trivial of matters.

Regardless of the chaos and hatred around us - that which we cannot fathom - we believe we know what love is. We are not aware of having placed layers upon layers of lies over the reality of love, even though we commonly mistake it for lust. In truth, we rarely experience true love and are therefore only familiar with a tiny representation of it that we render conditional. But love's power is so vast and infinite that even the slightest glimpse leaves us with a never-to-be-forgotten sensation of wellbeing. That we reinterpret this tiny peek into all sorts of nuttiness is no surprise given that the liar in our minds is still very much in residence.

The idea that we know everything already is a liar-mind perspective not limited to non-beneficial ideas. The liar's distortions will shift and swirl in any direction in order to manipulate perception to its own design. It becomes fiercely inventive in order to regain the control of minds which were lost to it briefly while witnessing true love, even if just for a nanosecond. This unbiased inventiveness explains the most outlandish justifications for destructiveness in so-called spiritual settings.

The defiance of the liar within purported *loving* environments is therefore no surprise. Maintaining the belief in separation and isolation ensures that even in *loving* and *spiritual* settings there will be continued misinterpretation. One of the most spurious of these misinterpretations, witnessed in many disingenuous cults and sects, is the insistence that any sort of behaviour is reasonable. To arrive here, forgiveness must be redefined as excusing behaviour, and so we are diverted from witnessing the true nature of our insanity and the suffering it causes. This must be a liar-mind tactic because seeing the problem clearly and so understanding it will ensure its elimination, and it can't have that.

Even more tricky misrepresentations of forgiveness may arise after we have accepted that the world in which we live is a surreal dream. From here, some deceitfully argue that whatever we do here is of no importance. This argument has already confused dispassionate examination with condemnation, and thus redefines forgiveness as apathy. It can only come from a mind that has not yet been able to look dispassionately and so still cherishes condemnation, but refuses to admit this. This mind that believes it understands forgiveness actually does not want to look at anything at all and would rather hide under the bedclothes and let the madness continue, shouting all the while: *It doesn't exist. It doesn't exist!* When asked to look at a particular *unforgivable*, this state of mind is unable to avoid becoming agitated and confused, as it has not approached true forgiveness in any real sense; rather, it has avoided it.

Faith in the innocence of the human race ensures that, when we do look at our lunacy, we are never alarmed or frightened. Those who use the *world is illusion* argument to avoid accepting our insanity, insist we do not need to look carefully at our behaviour in order to forgive it, but often become confused and defensive when asked to consider a certain aspect of our madness. This blindness can do nothing to stop violence and suffering in the world.

To see the illusion truly is to first look at it without condemnation. When we look on the most appalling activities with no belief in sin or guilt, we can see how everything humans have ever done has been inevitable. We have not known what we were doing or why, and that is all. Shutting our eyes tightly, putting our fingers in our ears and making a loud noise to drown out reality is part of this not knowing what we do. When we dare take a peek, our fear has not dissipated any, and we are still deeply discomfited by the rage of our brothers. Recognising that the monsters we thought we saw in the dark are just helpless figures behaving insanely is the undoing of hallucination; not throwing ourselves under the covers to hide from it.

The *world is illusion* argument that assures us we don't have to look at anything closely means we would be right to tell a person with a broken arm not to worry because it is all just illusion. Surely, this is the same misstep made in karma cultures that justifies ignoring our brother bleeding in the gutter, given that it his karma and we must not get in the way of that. Yes, illusion = guilt = karma; one and the same.

An even more disturbing twist of meaning we make under the liar's orders, is the same argument just mentioned turned on its head. As the only reality is love, everything must be love, and thus all the chaos, war, and hatred in the world must be love too. This is rather illogical given the previous statement that everything in the world is illusion, as if illusion and truth could sit side-by-side with any comfort. This argument allows us to re-label fear as love, as well as justifying apathy and disinterest in the lives of our brothers. Looking at our errors and becoming inured to them is not part of forgiveness either.

We will find minds not yet able to accept their own insanity confusing any beneficial idea in order to reinterpret it for the liar's benefit. In truth, the illusion of the world can have some benefit for us if we can change our minds about its meaning and so allow our new view to help us to freedom. However, we do not see this loving benefit when we make the error and is never the intention behind the error either.

We cannot win with the duality machine interpreting for us; this liar which we have not yet noticed, even at the highest levels of the current spiritual evolution movement. We will talk about love, peace, and unity consciousness without having uncovered the false thinking we have cherished for eons and, for that reason, we are bound to make mistakes in our assessment of freedom. This is why we might go to a meeting that promises to free our minds and find ourselves sleepily parting with our life's savings. It is why we might connect with a group that promises eternal happiness but very quickly find ourselves in yet another shallow, emotionally dependent relationship and pretty miserable too. We might believe that free sex is the way to nirvana, without having noticed this behaviour is, in truth, refusing to let go of a lower evolutionary state of mind that serves us no loving purpose. We might be persuaded into believing we will find freedom through drug taking, such a belief held dear, even after decades of failure.

It is no wonder we are still so confused, even after decades of self-help, therapy, yoga, and healing practices. The truth is, while the liar is unrecognised, we won't want to change, and we won't desire peace either and, on top of it all, we won't realise that we won't. The liar is deciding for us and we believe what it tells us. On one level, we are aware that the world, as it is, is not what we want. We moan and complain about it continuously. Whenever we are offered a chance to change, we usually only accept a part of the healing, keeping intact that suffering which sits well with the liar's definition of how things should be for us personally; and we see this suffering as our joy.

We are rarely prepared to let go of our universal dominion of all things. Doing so would be brave surrender and we are certainly not ready to let go of romance, sex, and all our other special relationships. We are not ready to welcome our brother into our hearts either. Because if we were, we would see his suffering very clearly and we would jump to his aid immediately by understanding it to be our own suffering too.

When we know that we are one with all humanity, we cannot ostracise or ignore other people's distress; it doesn't matter how near or far away we are from each other. Due to this, if an opportunity arises to help our brother in pain, we must take it, whether we are successful or not. Also, we must not insist on helping if there is no request. Neither do we consider ourselves *better* than him and so able to *heal* him. The perceptual healing we all must undertake is personal work. True healers are those who provide the circumstances in which others may do their own healing. True healers don't need a magic wand, or odd sounding words, or a strange machine with flashing red lights. We are our own healers.

When the dark fog of lies believed begins to disperse, the light of truth will start to shine through; but not before. When we start eliminating fear from our thoughts, we cannot help but notice we are one with all human beings; indeed all life. It was only fearfulness that kept us separate, lonely, and isolated. From a loving perception our togetherness is undeniable. This togetherness is never a dubious notion of love which appears to be more like selfish bliss; especially when it excludes by maintaining separateness, preferring to turn its eyes away from the pain of our fellows. Even though pain is indeed illusion, while any human being believes it is real, his mind remains in slavery and there is work to do.

We remember the days in which our minds were permanently entwined in knots of condemnation. We recall year on year of grudge holding; the rolling mind never ceasing in its retelling of the same old story of persecution. We can even laugh now at how lost we used to be. Occasionally we are blessed with a glimpse of truth so dazzling we feel reassured that we have found our true path. Even so, every now and then, we will stumble or crash into condemnation and fear by the most nonsensical of situations. Our work is unfinished and, while the world is as it is, our work remains unfinished, because this is the liar's world.

Even with a steady spiritual practice, things must be the way we wish them to be. Because we do seem to be completely isolated and alone in our bodies, it is not too difficult to infer that - at the very least - our personal world must be governed by ourselves. And what other world is there, given we are the most important person around? We project our perceptual rulership into the external world and onto the people around us, as per the liar's decree. Usually, we find our attempts to control thwarted at every turn. Nevertheless, we continue to believe that we are absolutely right to insist on things going our way. No matter how many times we are blocked, we still believe we are right.

We must control the world. That is what a person does who is being constantly reminded, and so believes, that she is the sole ruler of the cosmos, the only important one, the only one who matters. Every *unforgivable* we have just looked at stems from this mad belief because our way is always the *right* way, even when it is outrageously savage. We should be the winner and have the most things. We should be able to dispatch the others with the most ease. We do not notice our deep depression and fear, but it is showing on everyone's face. We rarely smile, and there is little lightness or joy in our expressions; especially in the West where we all look terrified. We reveal fear and closed-heartedness in our countenance and mannerisms that we have learned from recurring and incessant attack and defence experiences.

We share everything; the good, the bad, the ugly. Once we see this clearly, forgiveness becomes a breeze. How could we not behave the way we do given our shared consciousness and the destructive beliefs we have never questioned? We have all been suffering from the same diseased perception, and condemning the insane is never justified because the insane do not know what they do. Without this new, easy concept of forgiveness, we will continue to think we know what love is, while continuing to mistake it for lust. We will not begin to question our thoughts and so will rarely see their destructive nature. We will believe we are able to forgive, yet will become decidedly uncomfortable when someone mentions an *unforgivable*. Even more bizarrely perhaps, we will continue to be totally unable to forgive our best friend for having done something ridiculously meaningless.

When we believe we have understood the mechanics of forgiveness and are still unable to apply them successfully to our best friend, we must have misunderstood something key along the way. We might be able to forgive the dastardly behaviour of notorious villains but if we become angry and resentful because our best friend never pays for a drink - or some such trivia - we didn't solve any problem at all. Forgiveness, as we now redefine it, must solve all problems, however big or small they seem to be. There is no order of difficulty in forgiveness. The truth is, our best friend is Hitler and our best friend is Jesus Christ, and our best friend is everyone in between too.

If we find ourselves struggling, it is usually with that which we have yet to forgive in ourselves. For example, I found it fairly easy to forgive men their belief in the need for violent and aggressive behaviour when I saw it for the lie that it is. This is because I had not received these self-identifiers myself, outside of my attempts to *succeed* in a world which required me to take on these characteristics. I found it far less easy to forgive a close friend her inability to see why viewing herself as a sexual object for sole use by violent men is a self-destructive thought pattern. This is because I also had identified with this false thinking for many decades and undoing it in my own mind took some work. Once I realised that I am as insane as my friend - and how could I not be under the circumstances - it was easy to let go. However, that didn't mean I found myself able to condone such thinking; not at all. Instead, I stopped feeling angry about ignorance I'm unable to do anything about and removed myself from this particular ward of the institution we all live in; one I had been hanging out in for way too long.

Spurious notions of forgiveness might suggest there is nothing wrong with these destructive beliefs but any belief based on separation is an obstacle to love, whatever it is and however much we cherish it. We might struggle to discard these beliefs, using misinterpreted forgiveness in order to deviously keep them, but all separating ideas are the same and none of them has any value at all. We are just time-wasting.

Letting go of the condemnation of the lost does not mean we have to continue to socialise superficially with them and suffer their madness. But we will understand why they are the way they are because we were with them there, not so long ago. This knowledge does not obstruct our love for them either. From understanding comes compassion. I remember very well when I was as lost, scared, depressed, and alone and so I honour anyone's choice to live in darkness while it remains appealing. Furthermore, although these loved ones are deeply unhappy and don't realise why they are, it is not my place to rework their stories for them. I'm sure there are elements of liar madness remaining in my own mind that those less afflicted than I will not be able to indulge either. I would hope to be pulled up on them too. The work must come from within. We are our own healers and, when we are ready to heal, everything we need will be provided. But it is ultimately our own choice.

We must surrender to the process of life, wherever it may take us, assured that truth will find us when we stop insisting on defining it for ourselves. Until then, forgiveness will be limited to that which we feel no fear in examining. If fear arises when we are asked to forgive, we can be sure we are cherishing one of the liar's ideals. Our relative attachment to the idea will signify the intensity of defence we raise against unveiling it. Any defence is an attack, however seemingly insignificant the matter. The quietest, *No I didn't!* can be felt like a knife in the heart and, until we can see why the mind is so quick to defend itself, irrationally and illogically, we will be seduced into reacting angrily, defending ourselves absurdly, and maintaining this world of conflict.

While we endure pain, guilt, and an inability to forgive our nearest and dearest, how can we possibly forgive the unforgivable? Yet, if we know about this liar and how its ideas are not our own; if we witness its workings that appear rather like an unemotional software virus; if we see that our mind simply needs a scan and a clean; we can devote another part of our mind to the virus scanning function. This scanning is an attempt to catch all thoughts before we believe them; checking whether they are our own or not. The liar's patter continues and to suggest it hasn't without having levitated, or something like that, is another lie. While we are here, the liar will be ferreting away, seeking out conflict and attempting to incite it. Our job is to notice it first and never give it credence. That's all we have to do.

Can you imagine a couple who decide to do the work together talking a few years from now: *Honey, I just had the most ridiculous idea about you? Oh yeh, what was that? You know, I thought I saw something in your eye while you were talking to the neighbour when he came round just now. Oh, yeh, that's so insane, isn't it? But, actually, you know what; I did have that thought you saw, just now when the neighbour came round. Yes, lust wafted through my awareness. I noticed it. I was thinking; wow, there it is again, that crazy mind. Yeh, honey, wow.* And then these two will look at each other and start laughing, uproariously, tears rolling down their cheeks. They will laugh like a teenager does, the first time he smokes pot with his friends. They will laugh like this because it will be nonsensical to think we could actually betray each other in this way; the way we currently do on a daily basis, believing it to be real.

It is, in truth, hilarious that we should be suspicious and crazy like we are. And all it takes to see the comedy is to stop believing the fundamental ideas. That's it; so easy. These two will be having an experience of true relationship by having first understood exactly which thoughts are not their own. The will bring up every fearful thought they notice, question it and discard it. And every time they are fearful, they will sit quietly together to scan their thoughts and uncover any belief not yet revealed as untrue. Once we see that a belief we have is false, we can catch it more easily the next time it flies by; as it undoubtedly will while the liar remains in residence, albeit steadily running out of steam.

In any case, although a bit silly, this label of best friend is ridden with lies in that it singles out one person for special treatment over all the others. Whenever we do that, we suffer; because this person can never be what we have made them to be in our minds. They will eventually disappoint us because whatever we made of them is illusory. It will never be them; our *best friend* is a phantom. The truth is, everyone is our best friend and no-one any better than the rest. This is life without the liar and the beginnings of the saving of our world.

23 THE END'S BEGINNING

Once upon a time, a famous composer wrote a piece of music that was so far outside the human collective consciousness' definition of normality at the time, it sparked a riot when it premiered in Paris in 1913. Stravinsky's orchestral ballet, *The Rite of Spring*, provoked such an intense emotional reaction in the audience, the music became inaudible due to the uproar, and the crazed audience even threw chairs around. This was not the same sort of irritation we feel when we hear banal Bieber ditties; no, this was more like an audience meeting alien beings on the musical stage. The newness shocked and terrified them, sending them into a tizzy. They did not know what they were doing.

At varying levels of intensity, this is how we all tend to react when deeply held and cherished lies are suddenly and unexpectedly questioned for truthfulness. We believe the liar's thoughts are our own, so whenever its ideas are cross-examined, it senses attack and this fear of attack transfers onto our erroneous self-identification with it. We believe we are being personally attacked too. Notice that it is only the lies we cherish that cause us disgruntlement when challenged. When we are able to discard them, we stop reacting angrily whenever something challenges them. But whenever we must defend these false positions, the intensity of our defensiveness can get out of control and cause us to act destructively and regrettably.

Although we are not consciously aware of the lie of separation, the liar insists we defend it constantly and, in order to do so, we use obvious or subtle differences as proof of separateness. The most powerful lie we all believe is that we are separate from each other, completely isolated, alone, lonely, and unable to communicate from within our tiny, vulnerable bodies. This lie is so ingrained in our thoughts, we rarely notice it is just an idea. That every idea we have is shared, we notice even less frequently.

The *all we are is a body* lie has never been brought to question, just like many other incontestable lies we believe. If we look back at some of our major perceptual achievements in the last century we will see that it is in uncovering lies about each other and discarding them where we have found the most peace. Those false ideas had never previously been questioned for truthfulness and so caused us much pain.

We may believe in the equality of all human beings but, if we remain unaware of a deeply held belief, just like those deleterious ideas we believed for eons, how might we be able to discard it? Even the *religious*, the *holy*, and the *righteous*, century by century, have proved themselves as insane as everyone else. And how can they not have been, given that the problem itself has evaded awareness.

The human mind is mostly unchartered territory because the loudest voice residing within it requires us to remain ignorant of it. Even so, the obvious is staring us in the face and it just takes a quiet glance with an open mind to see everything in a different light. One obvious truth is that, because we are able to communicate with each other, this necessarily means we share ideas and conscious thoughts. The ability to communicate is our gift as humans and means that minds are connected, not separate.

The connections that we make via consciousness are relationships with each other, regardless of how long or short they may appear to endure over time. Understanding that we are all in relationship with each other, constantly, unceasingly, is the key to freedom from separation. Yet, as long as we believe we are separate from each other, in any sense at all, our experience of true relationship will be pitiful.

Conscious collective communication can be seen in other species on the planet, for example in ant and bird communities - I'd love to know what the parrots are chattering about so zealously even though I'm sure it's not particularly interesting. However, the human being is the only species which has taken this communication function to its logical conclusion. It is only the human that may free the mind from the belief in the physical boundary as prison and nihilistic destiny. Today, with the resources and opportunities at hand, we have projected the truth of our connectivity into the external world in the form of telecommunications and the Internet. This is the task of the human being; to take consciousness to the next level, and understanding that we are in constant relationship with each other is what it is all about.

When we who have believed in our separation, our superiority, and our inferiority for eons hear that nothing divides us apart from false ideas, we may initially react like the audience at the Théâtre des Champs-Élysées a century ago. In fact, this is to be expected. We will bitterly, and maybe violently, defend our right to remain the top dog, and our right to remain the persecuted underling, until we can see that these ideas have no value and only serve to support suffering in the world. We may expect men to become enraged or offended when told that the beliefs they have accepted without question since birth are the aggressive labels that must inevitably lead to war, violence, and the abuse of women across the world. Those men that feel they would not behave in such a way, and are deeply distressed and offended by the suggestion they are just like the mad rapist, have missed the point entirely. We use extreme examples beside subtle ones to point out that one error is the same as any other and that what our brother does in desperation and fear, we would also do given the same set of circumstances and beliefs.

We may attempt to defend these self-identifying labels as normal - boys will be boys maybe - without having first seen that this way of thinking was inherited and not decided upon personally, and can equally be discarded. We never accepted willingly and consciously the labels with which we define ourselves; they were instead dumped on us. Defending violent masculine labelling as natural and reasonable is like insisting an amphibian, with the potential to breathe air, should stay under water. It is illogical and stuck fast in an unwillingness to change.

On the other hand, we may expect women to become enraged and offended that we have suggested that the worship of the masculine deity is unfounded and perilous. More likely, we may expect women to misinterpret this message of connection, love, compassion, and equality as an incitement to bitterness and rage at the perceived persecution and mistreatment of the female over the ages. But harbouring anger is a way of avoiding the fact that we have only been doing what we know and we have known little else until very recently. Misinterpretation and angry reactions are expected but, as with Stravinsky's *Rite Of Spring*, these new, peaceful and, at first, shocking ideas will hopefully take root and find firm footing in human consciousness. The results of changing our collective mind on so many deeply held beliefs will give us what we have been crying out for, ever since we can remember.

Beneath the incessant chattering of the liar are its *givens* we rarely get to see. These are the ideas it has implanted in our minds from birth and are so well established it does not have to repeat them loudly. The chatter we might more easily become aware of is, in fact, second-order nonsense. Uncovering the superficial ideas, which are usually specific to us personally, does not pose much of a threat to the liar. The *givens* that we must undo, lying just beneath all this petty noise, we rarely noticed. Eventually, a sincere willingness to be open-minded enough to see the truth, as it is, will uncover them.

I saw one of these deep *givens* once, clearly, on a silent meditation retreat. On day six it whizzed by instantaneously. It was so fast, I nearly missed it. *There's something wrong with me*, I heard the liar whisper. Due to its speed, it nearly evaded my awareness, but my thought processes had already calmed to the point of being able to witness and examine it, before it got away. This was not a belief I had been aware of having but, after some reflection, I realised that it had indeed been informing my every step in the world. This belief was not personal to me, either; this one is a human *given*.

There is something important to be conscious of around uncovering these *givens*. We must be aware that sharing the experience with those who have yet to understand the liar, usually permits the liar in their minds to single us out as *different* again. We need to be prudent with how open we will be and we need to know our audience well. When I have spoken about uncovering the liar like this with friends, I have seen their eyes glaze over with pity, and some delight, at the idea they now owned a private thought of mine which they may hold against me at some time in the future. I realised, sadly, that the liar had successfully promoted separation again and communication was blocked. When we do not understand the liar well, talking about it can play into its hands. This is how it has managed to confuse the common label we use for it with all sorts of good things that it is not.

Revealing a lie we once believed gives the liar a good reason to single us out as worse-than, or poorer-than perhaps. This is a tricky area of the work. Some people are not ready to assimilate honest and open conscious awareness, and the stories we tell of our experiences in freeing ourselves from the grip of the liar-mind may well cause distress. We must ensure we don't frighten anyone, while avoiding a misrepresentation of victim or aggressor either. When we all are sure that what we are discussing is always false, this will become easier.

We would do well to remember that whatever we have thought ourselves to be, whoever we are, has been in error. When an inability to empathise puts distance between us, we are going in the wrong direction. When anger and bitterness arise at the examination of an idea that has caused much heartache, we would do well to remember to ask ourselves: *What am I protecting by this angry reaction?* Honest self-questioning can serve to bring us back to calmness and sanity, and thus to reversing whatever separating concepts we had just been fighting so intensely to uphold.

True relationship, which is intent on undoing the lies that cause us so much distress, is love. However, unsurprisingly, the liar reinterprets for us the ideas that support love and union. Sometimes these reinterpretations are less destructive than others. However, wherever we are on the path through our short lives on Earth can be beneficial for all. For example, sitting and meditating alone in a cave for decades leaves us little opportunity to cause havoc in the world. Even the Nazi madness, madness that went beyond anyone's comprehension or imagination, we can now use for our benefit by being the most extreme example of the liar's indulgence we will allow. We should be clear that there but for the grace of God go all of us in ignorance.

Even when it hurts, we should attempt to respond rather than react. We should remember that no-one, apart from a handful of holy people, has ever known what they were doing and that includes us too. Forgiveness means allowing the anger and fear to come up, but to be willing to observe it rather than let it overwhelm us and take control of our minds. When we are able to put the peaceful, watching mind between the liar's ideas and our experience of life, we are finally able to see the madness that has engulfed us for what it is; madness. This is forgiveness.

Until the liar in the human mind is understood, if we have true faith in the innocence of our human sisters and brothers we may find ourselves able to let go of condemnation. But we will not have understood the problem itself and so will usually have to repeat the exercise. True faith is the experience of a very small number of deeply spiritual human beings on our planet, and I believe we need something rather more accessible and unquestionable that requires no spiritual faith. This way, freedom is not limited to those members of a particularly labelled group, and so remains open to all seven billion of us.

Forgiveness means halting judgment and condemnation before we believe it to be justified. Forgiveness means being aware of the insanity of the human mind and so assuming we have rarely made the right decision. Forgiveness is not claiming to be free of condemnation, while holding onto a small place in our hearts in which we still consider *evil* real. We don't forgive something and then keep on having to forgive the same thing, again and again.

While we continue to have to forgive the same thing, over and over again, we are making life unnecessarily difficult for ourselves. While we are here on Earth, the liar is still in residence in the mind; careening about, reminding us of the persecution or the insult, and duping us into agreeing with it repeatedly. However, freedom shouldn't be hard work - that's another oxymoron - and if the journey seems overly unpleasant we might have made a wrong turn somewhere. That's not to say that undoing a lie will be a nice experience, because it usually won't. However, if we are not having regular joyful periods, which are becoming longer and more enduring, we might need a rethink on our personal definition of forgiveness.

Things that remain outstanding in the forgiveness stakes are the things we daren't look at calmly and dispassionately, mainly because we are too frightened to do so. We are scared that if we look closely enough, we will see that we have been very wrong about ourselves. This sets the liar off in the mind, causing us deep distress and an inability to think rationally and logically. We become enraged when it is suggested that we could have been so wrong, for so long.

The courageous among us will take that first step, however; taking a deep breath and jumping fearlessly into the abyss. While there, although terrified, they will see that what they thought was unquestionable was actually a load of nonsense. Hell's looming monstrousness will dissipate and the horrors of the world will be seen to be the inevitable result of a mind at war with itself. And once the looking and discarding has commenced in earnest, nothing can remain hidden or buried deep in our shared consciousness, waiting to pounce and cause us pain in an instant. As Byron Katie says: *An uncomfortable feeling is not an enemy. It's a gift that says, 'Get honest. Inquire'.* It is through the honest and courageous inquiry of everything that troubles us that we will find freedom.

There is still much work to do before we will release ourselves from mental slavery. *Unforgivables* abound in the world and there are many more events requiring a chapter in this book. Perhaps we could consider a second edition together in which you might like to collaborate with me on forgiving the unforgivable. Perhaps we could rewrite the whole book again, each chapter taken on by someone closer to the subject. This might be especially useful if it transpires that people have become angry with lil' ole me for having had the nerve to tackle issues of which I have had no personal experience; although that is clearly a liar idea, firmly rooted in the belief in separateness and the inability to understand one another.

Certain situations, like the stolen children of the native Australians, or the abuse arising from the Indian caste system, for example, remain outstanding. As always, the underlying cause comes from the better-than beliefs of some which insist on the worse-than-ness of others. When a group of people are considered less-than, in any sense, we are compelled to treat them badly in order to attempt to mitigate our guilt for having assumed them as such. The circularity of our reasoning and the fact that our guilt is never mitigated - instead growing steadily with each new destructive act - means the chaos continues to spread, getting out of control.

The liar will persuade us not to look at the state of the world, no matter how strong our spiritual practice is or how dedicated we are. Instead, we will be convinced to indulge in the feelings of peace and love we find in our spiritual practice in isolation, disregarding anything we might be able to do for the rest of humanity. This is hypocrisy.

We might have noticed the beneficial changes of mind we have made in the last few hundred years that have brought more peace to our world. This peacefulness has crept up on us without us noticing and is probably not recognised as exceptional by the younger generation. This is the forgiveness we are talking about here; brought to us by the brave defenders of reality, against all odds. If we consider the continued abuse of the feminine, or the outrageous activities of corporate monsters, or the racist thinking of lunatics to be none of our business, we have missed the point entirely.

As long as anything remains unforgivable, the liar's world is intact and the human mind exists in darkness and ignorance without knowing that it does. Yet, given that we are even talking like this, must suggest that optimism for the future isn't entirely unfounded. We have had enough now, surely. It is time to wake up.

A loving heart generates words and actions that can have unlimited beneficial effects in the world. A loving heart, that has not singled out this love for anyone one person or group of people specifically, may extend its warmth to all. And there is no limit to the power of love. Like the chaotic butterfly's wing, one generous and unexpected smile could inspire someone to do something they hadn't previously considered. This unplanned action could have a knock on effect, like miraculous dominoes, which may, perhaps, stop a war starting far away across the planet. Being sure that our loving heart can produce benefits such as these gives us good reason to carry on.

Even love not based on sex is now recognised a little. In our afflicted world, in which the most unusual thing we might have said to each other for eons is *I love you*, love is finally breaking into mainstream thinking. This is a very recent event. My father, whose own father was born in Victorian times, winces whenever I tell him I love him; and so I tell him as much as I can and the wincing has become less severe. Even in the recent Star Wars epic, the *force* is never called love, although love is all it could be. I noticed that throughout the films the word *love* is not mentioned at all outside of romantic relationships. These films are barely ten years old and yet we all understand now that *love* is something much bigger than whatever we used to believe it to be. Perhaps we realise we want it as much as it wants us, and perhaps we are accepting that it can be an integral part of our lives too.

At each step of conscious evolution, we become more peaceful and less fearful. Perhaps we could say that some of us are now experiencing 2% of the truth instead of the 0.00001% of which the rest of the world is aware and so too our own cultures not so long ago. Our religions have always described God as being far, far away and un-contactable. Perhaps, as we close in on the truth, we will close in on Him too. Still, while the majority of our thoughts are lies, we will not be able to understand love, fearlessness, or true peace. The work is uncovering what we have placed in the way of truth due to the inevitable mistakes we have made; the erroneous beliefs that came from earlier, more fearful evolutionary states; the beliefs that had stuck like glue in our minds before we were even human and so have never been brought to question. As we discard the lies and so shift our perspective, our experience of life will approach that of Heaven.com; our true home. Evolution is a matter of decision.

Remember: this liar we are talking about is nothing at all; it cannot exist because everything about it is untrue. There is nothing we can pin down as genuine inside its functionality. It is entirely unreasonable. Even so, while we believe its ideas, its effects in the world appear very real indeed. Here, we are just usefully giving it a name and description while we set about dismantling it. There will be shifts and re-shifts in perception as we find a way to incorporate a new and beneficial belief in the equality of all humans; life without the liar.

The arrival of a collective state of mind in which fear cannot exist is plainly inevitable. This may, however, take some time; but we can be sure it will arrive. Until enough of us are on-board, *nothing left to lose* will have been one of the best places to be for a clearer view on reality. When there is nothing in the world to keep us here, we might then see the unattached truth of what we are. This has been the experience of some of our greatest, modern, spiritual leaders and thinkers who have arrived at peace only after profound suffering.

We are only alone if we believe we are separate and isolated inside a body. Our tiny separate being can do nothing on its own, but together we are invulnerable and miracles should be commonplace. We will not be free of suffering until we have forgiven everything, and properly. Ultimately, nothing is, in fact, *unforgivable*; we have simply been in error. Understanding the error will eradicate the need for more unforgivable-type behaviour and spiritual apathy will be revealed as the hypocrisy it is.

Knowing that the process of evolution has been moving steadily towards relationship and connectivity leaves us unable to deny our insanity any longer. We see that the fear that has motivated our every step for millions of years was just a mistaken belief in separateness. Nothing will remain unforgivable, and nothing will remain hidden deep inside the mind when we are not frightened of it any longer. Furthermore, nothing can remain unhealed when we are able to accept our personal responsibility for the problem. All our pain and suffering has just been part of the crazy and inevitable mess we have made with our mistaken beliefs. Being unable to forgive is like insisting that the person or people we cannot forgive should be Buddha already.

We have been looking at the results of our problem and confusing the results with the problem itself. It is as if we burnt the bread and then blamed it on the crust. That is how mad we have been. The problem is with us alone; the thoughts playing inside each and every one of our minds. Step one is admitting the problem.

When we notice how angry we have been at the world and how we have harboured a conviction that only *other people* do all the bad stuff, but never us, we would do well to look around and see that we all share the same thoughts. We pick out our *bad guys* while we will be the *bad guy* to someone else; roles changing and shifting incessantly. In truth there are no bad guys, only good ones. Our world seems to be inequitable from top to bottom, yet every idea that supports the inequality is a lie. And if that's not good news, I don't know what is!

The children are still running towards the fire though, their pace increasing. We do our best to stop them and avert them from doom; but we must face the fact that they may insist on running into the fire, no matter what we do. We may have to watch them destroy themselves repeatedly but we also must respect the decision making capacity of our equals, however faulty. Yet, while the insanity continues, we can be sure the insane will change their minds eventually. It is only a matter of time.

The guilt we have wrestled with, ever since we became aware, has also been inevitable. Our awareness approaches the knowledge of what we truly are; peaceful, loving, compassionate, and kind. With these inklings of what we are, in truth, all behaviour we brought with us from past evolutionary states reeks of guilt because it is very fearful. Treating our brothers and sisters as if they were nothing, or owned, or the owner, in the same way the animal world does, naturally invokes guilt on a being who is conscious of the true noble state of all humanity. We are already half aware of what we are and, because of this, we must experience guilt. Any action based on fear is an abomination on the truth of our being. Guilt has been utterly unavoidable.

How could we not have been guilty, having a sure notion of what we are in truth? How could we not feel sadness and pain, as we hurt ourselves by hurting our brothers and sisters? How could we not have continued with our destructive actions, having brought the liar with us into awareness from lost, terrified, and filthy earlier stages of life on Earth? We have had to experience guilt because on becoming human we became aware of what we are. We cannot hide from the brilliant truth of our being; that which is peaceful, loving, and kind. We have never been able to hide, not really. Hiding from our true selves gave rise to the guilt which has fuelled the liar ever since its inception.

Eliminating lies from our perception leaves us light and happy. We cannot look at each other in error again. Having discarded guilt from our thinking, we find ourselves able to focus all our time on beneficial activities. We are content, finally. Our hearts are open. The peace for which we have been searching eternally has arrived. From here, who knows what we will do next. Our options are now unlimited and blessings might be our trade. Whatever we do next remains to be seen, but whatever is to come will be the brilliant side effects of our work in discarding the liar from our collective consciousness.

At the foundation of our glistening future will be peace, and freedom from the pain, suffering, and frustration we accepted as a normal part of life. We must remain alert however. If this new freedom coming from the forgiven human mind cannot be transferred to everything and anything that has ever caused us pain then it is not true freedom and the liar will still be floating around somewhere.

We are welcome to believe in the veracity and importance of the shadow, of the darkness, of the liar, for as long as we like. That is our prerogative. But the darkness only seems to be real prior to escaping it. Just before we see the light, we may believe the darkness to be forever inescapable, but this is defeatism not coming from our own true and brightly lit mind. Whenever we experience true healing, we know without doubt that the darkness and pain we had been sure was real was, in fact, illusion. Amazingly, the liar manages to persuade us of the reality of sin even after we proved it false in this way. Our choice of shadow or light, sin or innocence, defines the world we build for the liar or the world we create for purified humanity. But, whatever we believe, our light is eternal; it will never go out.

In forgiving the unforgivable, we brought the light of knowledge to the dark places we had saved for condemnation in our collective consciousness. When the light of truth was brought to the darkness, the darkness was unable to withstand it and disappeared. We will bring any more shadows in our minds to light, clarity, and reason in the same way, and these shadows will disappear too. We will see that we could have only ever believed in *darkness, sin,* and *evil* prior to examining our thoughts for truthfulness and discovering we have been in error. We will finally see that the light of truth has never had an opposite. It can *only* be One.

And now, the madness of it all is clearly seen.
And where is importance to be found, within a dream?
All things that once made sense have fizzed away,
Those things that urged me onward, day to day.
And now, there is but knowing, all this will pass.
And in the meantime, what to do? I can but ask.
While sifting through the wreckage of thought gone wrong,
I wonder if I hear correctly, this new song.
I know that You may speak to me, as plain as day.
From what you've told me, here and there, when'er it mattered.
Why not to be so close continuously?
Why linger on in this asylum without doors?
Please show me how to leave, and so be done.
Please show me, that I too might show someone.

Printed in Great Britain
by Amazon